Cursillo

ANATOMY OF A MOVEMENT

THE EXPERIENCE OF SPIRITUAL RENEWAL

MARCENE MARCOUX

LAMBETH PRESS
NEW YORK, NY

© 1982 by Marcene Marcoux. All rights reserved.
Printed in the United States of America.

Library of Congress Cataloging in Publication Data

Marcoux, Marcene.
  Cursillo, anatomy of a movement.

  Bibliography: p.
  Includes index.
  1. Cursillo movement.   I. Title.
BX2375.A3M26   269.6   81-20704
ISBN 0-931186-00-5   AACR2

LAMBETH PRESS 143 E. 37th St. New York, NY 10016

DEDICATION

To my parents
Cora and Laurier Marcoux
for whom having daughters
was never second best.

CONTENTS

Preface vii

Part I: Description of the Cursillo
    1. The Struggle to Exist   3
    2. Preparation and Training for Initiation   35
    3. Living Cursillo   65
    4. The Fourth Day:
       Conversion and the New Community   101

Part II: Analysis of the Movement
    5. Applauds and Assaults:
       A Deeper Look Within   133
    6. Catholicism and its Discontents   163
    7. Charisma and Tradition:
       The Creative Work of Renewal   191
    8. The Language of a Movement:
       On Speaking Cursillo   217

Appendix
    Methods and Assumptions:
    Turning the Periscope Inward   249

Bibliography   272

Index   287

PREFACE

T.S. Eliot's lines return:

What we call the beginning is often the end
And to make an end is to make a beginning.

The beginning of this book is truly an end. For only as I leave these words can you enter its world. Only in abandoning these pages, in their being pulled from the typewriter, can they be placed in your presence and in the unpredictability of your response.

It is at this point, in your going forward and in my withdrawing from the scene of this reading, that I reflect on the process of writing this book. It is the moment of looking back to those who have walked and talked with me, glances back to graduate school days to discussions, numerous and significant, with my teachers Johannes Fabian and Roy Wagner when all three of us were at Northwestern University; to my colleagues, Ray Baker and Julian Baird, who brought the sense that to teach was to speak in a voice both analytical and passionate, when we were teaching at Boston University. Looking back even further, and yet even closer, to my parents, Cora and Laurier, who stressed (at times not knowing the consequence) the significance of education; to my in-laws, who provided encouragement; and especially to Paul, my husband and friend, who gave warmth and love.

Can I really say thank you to all the others — to Jocelyn, Yvonne, Mark, and Aquinas — for living at the same time and sharing a history? Perhaps not, but I can say thank you for sharing your lives with me.

In a similar way, I wonder if one can thank the woods of Maine and the beaches of Nantucket for the spaces where I was able to reflect and think about thinking, for the excitement of a life lived and ideas teeming with the various seasons of these *wonder*ful spaces. These lands also are part of the process of this writing. I cannot thank the woods nor the beaches, but I can say I am most appreciative to those who first opened these worlds to me.

To members of the cursillo, those of you who told me your story and shared the depths of your religious experiences, I give you back pieces of yourself in a gilded mirror, to use if you want for decoration, as an artifact on your coffee table, or for the insights swirling within. For the poetry that surfaced in our interactions and for learning again that interviewing is human and open, I am most grateful.

For those of you now beginning to enter the world of the cursillo, may you find its path one that is both familiar and strange, both ordinary and extraordinary.

Marcene Marcoux

PART I

DESCRIPTION OF THE CURSILLO

CHAPTER 1

THE STRUGGLE

TO EXIST

Description of the Cursillo

Movements are fascinating phenomena. They involve beliefs and actions in the throes of social change and, as such, challenge the scientific concepts and paradigms generally applied to slower changing phenomena. By confronting movements, researchers are continually forced to reexamine the techniques and assumptions of their scientific craft. Because of this, the study of movements is ultimately a study of the methodology of the social sciences.

Social anthropologists have long been fascinated by movements. To be sure, a degree of our interest rests with the perspective that social movements are strange and unusual phenomena. Yet the degree to which movements such as the marching rule, kimbanguisme, or voodoo, for example, appear strange and exotic depends on our grasp of the possible range of social behavior as well as the actual phenomenon itself. To the extent that these movements shatter a researcher's expectations and conceptualizations of social action, these phenomena will appear unusual and puzzling.

Yet it should be remembered that one source of these expectations stems from the experiences and understandings of our own culture. And if there is one failing among anthropologists, it is the tendency to take our culture for granted. Too often we abandon in-depth investigations of American culture for the study of what are perceived to be more exotic cultures. It may be easier, and less anxiety provoking, to discover the exotic in a non-Western, preindustrial society, but certainly there is much in American culture that shatters our assumptions and expectations of human behavior when confronted.

Although there is not presently a phenomenology of the strange, anthropologists have followed Geertz's dictum that "the odd, strange and uncanny simply must be

The Struggle to Exist

accounted for."[1] Yet stalking the strange has frequently led anthropologists to discover the exotic as a dimension marking the ways of people different from ourselves. What this perspective does not encourage is the realization that the unusual is not just remote and existent "out there," but present within our culture and as close as the clothes we wear.

This study adjusts the periscope towards our own culture based, as it is, on the assumption that the exotic and the familiar are threads woven in the fabric of all societies. In this sense, it takes its starting point from a position phenomenologists have long held. "At bottom, the ordinary is not ordinary; it is extraordinary, uncanny."[2] Yes, we are all linked to, not separated from, people who join movements, be it the cursillo, the jamaa, the vailala madness, or pentacostalism. The sense of strangeness is what we share, and we are brought together by this very dimension. For in each culture and in every social situation, the curious and familiar are involved in an ongoing dialectic.

Only when we understand that the exotic is within us, as an inherent part of our culture, will we be able to handle the unusualness we perceive in others. Not to see this is to tame the alien, hoping perhaps to keep this dimension from surfacing. It is almost as if native and Third World people have served as projected images of the strange, allowing our strangeness to remain hidden. In doing so, we have not disturbed our consciousness, nor have we explored the terrain of our everyday world. We have acted as if the strange is apart from us, missing the significant realization that it is inevitably a part of us all.

To the extent that this research involves an examination of unusual language and behavior, it is a mirror of ourselves, a glimpse at the relationship between the ordinary and extraordinary aspects of social life. The cursillo is strange, as is the color of coffee, a handshake, the word *hello*. Sunbathing, collecting stamps, hitting a golf ball only make sense because we believe these activities to be common, ordinary, acts. Whether any of these are familiar or bizarre depends on whether we acknowledge, socially and historically, the sense-bestowing act of the object or event.

Since all activities are always in the process of making sense and losing sense, the cursillo struggles for understanding, competing with other activities to be considered meaningful and, thus, familiar. The reward of winning is being taken for granted; of losing, being labeled strange. This is the story of the cursillo: its successes and failures.

The question that first arises is not surprisingly: What is the cursillo? This question will recur, for there is no simple response. The cursillo possesses many angles and perspectives, and this research is a continual wrestling with that very question.

Briefly, the *cursillo de cristiandad* (literally, "short or little courses in Christianity") is a movement intent on renewing traditional Catholicism. Specifically, the renewal, as is the case in many movements, focuses on language. The cursillo's concern is the language of Catholicism; a speech perceived as archaic, marked by lifeless metaphors and ritualistic phrases, which produce a strained and artificial voice. The cursillo attempts to bring new life to this traditional language through a series of elaborate methods and approaches. As a movement, it is geared to rediscovering the meanings of early Christianity and, as such, is not revolutionary but radical because it goes to the root of the New Testament texts.

The Struggle to Exist

The cursillo fascinates because it is an attempt to fashion meaning and to revitalize both religious and social life. It is related to every other attempt to do exactly this: the cargo cults, the jamaa, the numerous monastic movements. To see the cursillo in this way is to focus on the related thread, the significant tie that it shares with movements in general: the urge to create, to forge powerful metaphors, and to shape images which call forth new designs for religious life.

The cursillo began as a journey to find the best words to convey the profound implications of the unspeakable, unutterable Word. This odyssey for a better language originated, however, not in the United States but in Mallorca. How did a small group on a resort island off the coast of Spain, reach so many people across different cultures? What do we know of these individuals whose ideas, in time, surfaced in a global religious movement? To discover these answers is to unravel the still tangled threads of the cursillo's beginning.

The history of the cursillo has inevitably framed its structure, directives, and method. Its origins in Mallorca have marked the movement; yet like the rocks that geologists believe "remember," the past "lives," but it lies hidden. Since the pathways backwards are not always evident, the history of the cursillo is not clear, but filled with contradictions, undisclosed influences, and political meddlings. Perhaps a movement that arises in Mallorca under the rule of Franco, in the midst of and following the ravages of the Second World War, and apart from the strict control of the Catholic hierarchy necessarily involves such a history. Thus what is presently known remains a series of pieces whose mosaic is still incomplete. Not all the pieces are in place; some may never be found.

Given these uncertainties, however, we do know with-

Description of the Cursillo

out doubt that the cursillo began at Mallorca. The when and how still remain clouded because the cursillo did not begin with a clean slate. No movement does. It came into existence with the attempt to organize a pilgrimage; this is not a revolutionary idea but part of Spanish Catholic tradition. The idea for a pilgrimage to the tomb of St. James the Greater occurred as a vague possibility in 1932; yet it was not achieved until 1948. Within this time and through the effort to organize the pilgrimage, the cursillo was formed. But the movement was an inadvertent result of the planning for the pilgrimage. So unexpected was the cursillo that the reality of its existence was not discerned by many people even when it was an ongoing phenomenon. Clearly, the cursillo originated as a process to organize, train, and enliven adolescents for a pilgrimage. It has now advanced to a method of renewing Catholic men and women throughout the world.

The large-scale plan for a pilgrimage to Santiago de Compostela engendered massive interest, and took years of preparation. During this time, courses were drafted to train leaders of the pilgrimages as some method was required to organize this imposing enterprise. The first courses were called the Cursillos of Pilgrim Scouts, and later the Cursillos for Pilgrim Captains were also formulated.

One of the men involved in these courses was Edouardo Bonnin. A simple and devoted man, he worked on these early teams and was part of the organization for the pilgrimage. Bonnin realized that something extraordinary occurred during those special courses: individuals became enthused, alive, and religiously motivated. Bonnin gained greater faith in this method and, through his own efforts, modified the courses towards a greater focus on personal faith and a renewed Christianity.

The Struggle to Exist

In many ways, Bonnin and the group of Mallorcan men reached out beyond their earlier plans. From the Cursillos of Pilgrim Scouts and the Cursillos for Pilgrim Captains, the courses evolved to include the Promoters' School and the Leaders' School until, by 1945, there was a vibrant atmosphere and a more elaborate method than had initially surfaced in the preparation for the pilgrimage. The courses that were established to turn adolescents into pilgrims had transformed the organizers into the first members of a movement.

By January 1949, it is clear that the cursillos were definitely separate from the preparation for the great pilgrimage that, after almost sixteen years of planning, had finally occurred in August of 1948. With seventy thousand pilgrims reaching Santiago de Compostela, the planning was concluded. Yet with the pilgrimage complete, the courses continued. Some in the early team of men experienced a shift in attitude, realizing as they did, that the significant pilgrimage was not the one to St. James the Greater but life itself. It was the pilgrimage of life one needed to prepare for and for which enthusiasm and joyfulness was necessary. In this way, the courses were recognized as serving a more enlarged and permanent audience. With this shift away from a more parochial perspective, the courses emerged in a more expansive light. Some men, such as Bonnin, saw this early. Others needed the completion of the great pilgrimage to grasp the latent function of the courses; and thus the cursillo held at San Honorato from January 7 to 10 in 1949 provided, for them, this first general awareness.

The history of the cursillo is the history of a realization, the process whereby individuals gain insight into the greater function of the cursillo, when they perceive, beyond the pilgrimage, a method of revitalization and of

Description of the Cursillo

triumphant Christianity. There is no first cursillo, just an awareness that occurs at different moments by some of the early founders when, for the first time, they understood the courses as a method of Catholic renewal.

The cursillo of January 7, 1949, is much heralded as the first cursillo; it may be, to the extent that most of the early members, including clerics, appreciated the more expansive role of the courses at this particular time. It stands as the occasion of a public recognition that the courses were more significant than previoulsy thought and that they held a promise not glimpsed years back. Bonnin, for one, understood this insight years before the cursillo at San Honorato.

It is clear that, as the course of Pilgrim Scouts and Pilgrim Captains progressed to include the Promoters' and Leaders' Schools, a vision was being glimpsed. From the structure and the talks, from the mobilization of individuals, there was some dimension beyond the pilgrimages emerging. It was now evident to some within this early Mallorcan team that here was a method of renewal, not only to usher in enthusiasm for a specific pilgrimage, but for life itself. From within this group, the carving of a vision and a method that could renew faith was slowly arising.

Bonnin, as a participant and formulator of the early courses, was one who appreciated quite early the potential of these courses. Exactly when this was apprehended is difficult to pinpoint, since there never is just one moment, but successive unravelings of a potential. However, we can say that by 1946 Bonnin considered these courses separately from the pilgrimage to Santiago de Compostela and as a force in their own right. Whether others in the team and within the Spanish Catholic hierarchy glimpsed this as early is not as evident. For many, the courses were aligned with a specific pilgrimage that would terminate with its completion. In the intervening years between Bonnin's understanding of the courses and the cursillo at San Honorato, others recognized the special quality of this method, created in their midst and fashioned by their combined efforts. By 1949, the vision of the courses as the cursillos, a method and a plan of renewal, was evident to the early Mallorcan team as it had been evident earlier to Bonnin.

What was it that Bonnin envisioned as he peered within the structure of the cursillo? What did he sense that would make this method something able to renew Catholicism? Clearly it pertained not only to his understanding of the method, but to his grasp of the direction and problems of the church itself. Certainly Bonnin realized that Catholicism was having its difficulties and not succeeding in many of its goals. In many ways, the Mallorcan church was wrought with problems related to the Spanish government and its fascist controls. Yet beyond this fact, there were other discontents with the present church orientation, and Bonnin knew that the church must change to be meaningful to its churchgoers.

Bonnin saw that religious success is never an accomplished fact since the church is an evolving process. From this perspective, he formulated the need for continual energizing of people, namely, renewal. Second, he noticed that religion had to be lived; it is not an intellectual fact and not necessarily a theology. Religion is based on faith, on the grasping of the inner vision of a powerful experience that alters one's world view. For Bonnin, the energy of the church must, in part, be directed not at theological reform but at getting the message of Christ to the people. Catholicism must be a living reality, a force that explodes and enlivens. He understood religion as not only belief and ritual; it is, at its core, an experience.

Description of the Cursillo

A third concern was the search for community. He caught sight of the essential social dimension to religious life, the need for social interactions and for the sense of a community wherein caring exists as a powerful force.

Fourth, because he clearly understood that faith is not self-sustaining, he realized that there is nothing inherent in faith that guarantees its continuation beyond the present experience. Where faith is the grasping of a hidden spirituality and the experience of unseen powers, it rests on a vision that can quickly dissipate. Faith thus demands a foundation for its continual renewal and for launching individuals on an ongoing search. Because Bonnin knew that faith is not empirical and is certainly not reinforced in a scientific and materialistic culture, he observed many forces turning people away from an intense faith. Thus, the church required a counter measure.

Bonnin accepted the premise that Catholics are not those who necessarily have faith, even though they may at one time have possessed faith. He noted the importance of conversion, not outside the church, but within. It was an insight that demanded the direction of the church's energy not only toward atheists and nonbelievers but also toward its own core of parishioners. Continual conversion of churchgoers rests on the idea that faith is not guaranteed with its first manifestation. This amounts to a distinct notion of religion based on conversion as a continual process.

This relates to his fifth insight, namely, that human beings are searchers and Catholics are continual pilgrims. He saw life as a journey that demands work and commitment, where people must learn to be active principals in the creation and shaping of their own lives, and in sustaining their religious experience. Faith is active, not passive, and the renewal of the church necessitates continual involvement.

Last, is his concern with what may be called the church's hermeneutics. Although Bonnin was convinced of the importance of the New Testament, he noted that it could not be assumed that Catholics knew these texts nor assessed them as significant. He felt that the church had to make the New Testament a true testament, conveying a live and dynamic worldview to transform believers at the level of their being.

These are but some of the insights Bonnin caught sight of in the very formation of the cursillo. For Bonnin, the cursillo had to be of a *vivencial* nature, leading to environmental transformation and existing in a lived experience of Christ. Given this, there was a role for accountability through a Christian community, which he was convinced the cursillo could structure and establish. A plan, rising from the insights and the work of the pilgrimage, had led to a course that could dramatically change lifeless Catholicism.

Yet while the pilgrimage was being planned and during the period when Bonnin came to frame the cursillo in a new light, an important factor occurred: a new bishop came to oversee the diocese of Mallorca. A bishop arrived who would become involved, at first inadvertently and later willingly, in directing the courses, preceding and following, the pilgrimage. Given his role in the hierarchical structure of the church, he would come, in time, to be ultimately responsible for the courses, having the final word in the direction of their evolution.

In 1947, Juan Hervas became the bishop of Mallorca, entering at the time of preparation for the pilgrimage, while its direction and method was still in process. Hervas's pastorship over Mallorca was historic for the movement and significant for him as a bishop. Hervas came when he was in his early forties, a priest who, like Bonnin

Description of the Cursillo

the layman, had certain discontents with Catholicism. He also had been aware of the church's lifelessness, the inactivity of parishioners, and their basic disinterest in Catholicism. Hervas himself instituted a plan for bringing life to his diocese and in time sought out individuals for what initially was a general proposal of renewal. Given the enthusiasm of the Catholic Action members that planned the pilgrimage, Hervas sensed in them a place to implement his ideas.

The courses for the pilgrimage, Bonnin's sense of this method as larger than the pilgrimage, and Hervas's idea of renewal intersected. The goals for change intertwined and the threads of various methods, of different personal objectives never disconnected. Hervas's designs, the work for the pilgrimage, and Bonnin's deep insight crosscut and fused. In this way, the cursillo was carved from the stone of all three quarries.

Hervas encouraged the courses for the pilgrimage preparation, definitely providing the early Mallorcan team with the legitimation to forge ahead. His acceptance of their methods added the needed reassurance while, unbeknown to them, their actions were perceived by Hervas as the result of his program for renewal. They rallied with his blessing and encouragement, yet their work was also the outcome of early efforts formulated without his presence. Certainly, Bonnin's insights were derived from an ongoing process that could have ceased had Hervas been antagonistic toward these courses. Without doubt, Hervas's arrival in Mallorca makes the history of the cursillo much more complicated, involving additional threads that today are still not separable, and making assessments of ownership difficult. Yet his presence eventually provided the cursillo with the catapult it needed to become an international movement.

The Struggle to Exist

Hervas was a person who, like Bonnin, possessed a vision. It involved a perspective of the church and a plan for action formulated before arriving in Mallorca, yet which took shape from the activities existing in his diocese. Hervas as bishop was entrenched in Spanish Catholicism, yet still critically aware of its existent problems. In many ways, Hervas identified the same issues Bonnin saw marking the church. Both men perceived the lifelessness of churchgoers, the insignificant mark of faith upon Christians in general, and the frequent apathy during liturgies. Within the writing of his texts, Hervas fashioned a picture of these problems, the perceptions that marked his childhood and his early years as a priest.

What is it that Hervas saw as the overwhelming problems of the church? The answer began when he was but eleven; he frequently attended Mass, yet was cognizant that somethings was missing. From an early age, Hervas was aware of the church's failure to move its members. The church seemed unable to induce excitement about Christianity, leaving many apathetic and uninvolved. On one particular occasion Hervas, moved by a powerful sermon, dejectedly realized that it was being heard by few parishioners. The church was empty, and its members were absent. Although only a boy of eleven, Hervas asked, "Why do so few people come to hear this man of God?" If the experience of Hervas when he was young is important, it is because this question continued to plague him throughout his life as a priest. Ordained when he was twenty-eight, he continually noticed that people were not hearing the Christian message, or if they were, they certainly were not responding. In one situation after another, Christians rejected their rituals and beliefs. Later, as a pastor of three parishes, Hervas again confronted the apathy of parishioners who did not attend

Description of the Cursillo

Mass and, when they did, experienced it as a lifeless performance. For many in his parish, Mass was a forced ritual attended out of fear of sin, not love. Hervas, as priest and pastor, continued to inquire, "Can it be that religion has no power or interest for the man of today?"

The lack of involvement in the church was also evident in another age group—the children and adolescents. As director of a reformatory, Hervas assessed the church's frequent failure to reach its younger members. His discussions with adolescents revealed their confusion and their alienation. Alone and afraid, they did not know where to turn. If this situation illustrates another failure of the church, it also reveals a comparable weakness in the family. Hervas comprehended the need for the family to be a cohesive unit wherein children, as well as parents, can work out personal and spiritual problems. The family, for Hervas, must be an expression of Christian love if the church is to succeed.

As Hervas changed roles and increased his responsibilities, he was constantly aware of the apathy, lack of concern, and at times, a general distrust of the church. Yet his various positions allowed Hervas to sense that his problems were not idiosyncratic, but representative of those of other priests in other locales. As one of the founders of the Council House of Catholic Action in Madrid (1933), he traveled throughout Spain, and his meetings with priests and seminarians confirmed what he saw in his own parishes. Since the Council House was charged with investigating apostolic activities, Hervas examined different organizational approaches used in Spain.

As a result of this investigation, Hervas witnessed the extent to which bureaucratic frameworks permeate religion. Catholic Action, seminarian, and diocesan organizations reflected the highly formalized structure of modern Catholicism. Aware of the great efficiency and control of such structures, Hervas however questioned the possible relationship between apathy and dissatisfaction of church members and organizational structures.

While active in Catholic Action, Juan Hervas attended the Inter-American Congress of Social Action in Cuba. Since the conference was relatively close to the United States, Hervas visited America. His travels in the United States took him through Toledo, Chicago, New York, Washington, and Boston, as he examined the organizational structure of the Catholic church in the States. His interest in social action led him to observe national religious organizations as well as local parish networks. His travels in the United States were brief, but they provided him with a firsthand observation of religious action groups in certain American cities.

In time, Hervas left Spain to attend the University of Frieburg, where he was particularly interested in pontifical documents. He researched the writings of various popes, especially Pius X and Pius XII. His study of papal documents led Hervas to conclude that many popes desired to renew the church and had searched for methods of revitalization. His research culminated in a thesis at the Faculty of Law of the University of Frieburg, "Hierarchy and Catholic Action in the Light of Law."

Impressed with Hervas's performance in his previous positions, members of the Catholic hierarchy first appointed him Vicar General and later Auxiliary Bishop of the diocese of Valencia, Spain. Then, after fourteen years in the priesthood, he was named Bishop of Mallorca, where he came in contact with the emerging courses, the early Pilgrim team, and Eduoardo Bonnin.

Hervas arrived in Mallorca with a readiness for change. He found a group in his diocese engaged in active

Description of the Cursillo

work; his plans and their actions coincided. He legitimized their innovation and encouraged their work even before he fully comprehended their specific ideas. At the crossroads were his designs for renewal and their work of training Christian leaders. The once separate paths fused; together they were directed toward the same goal of renewal. Hervas planned to use Catholic Action as a base for renewal, and many of the men preparing the pilgrimage belonged to this organization. It was the beginning of the sparks of change. The influence of one program upon the other would, in time, fan the fires of renewal.

For Hervas and many others, the signs of change were first evidenced at San Honorato in January of 1949. It was here the first cursillo is thought to have occurred: the weekend when the cursillo emerged as a method of renewal separate from the pilgrimages. Today there is a plaque at this monastery officially designating the events of that weekend as the birth of the cursillos. It is a date that many Spanish Catholic clerics are in agreement on. The question that arises is, What is at stake in labeling this weekend at San Honorato as the first cursillo? Why is this such a crucial question? Are there some hidden issues?

The question of San Honorato is one that sways the scales of judgment as to who was the true founder of the cursillo, Juan Hervas or Edouardo Bonnin. If the meeting at San Honorato is declared the first cursillo, then more credence can be given to the leadership of Juan Hervas and men like Juan Capo, the rector at that time. Hervas was the highest authority in the diocese and the one ultimately involved with overseeing this religious work. Credit can then be given to his position that the cursillo was the development of his pastoral plan and one of the

The Struggle to Exist

first steps in his idea for spiritual renewal. But if, as others admit, this was not the first cursillo but an extension of the courses begun before Hervas was ever in Mallorca, then there is more credence to Bonnin's role as the founder. Like the anthropologist in search of the missing clues, apelike man or manlike ape, much is at stake here. And the clues, as we know, are not free from biased interpretations.

According to Bonnin and Padre Segui, the cursillos as they are known today were well under way before Hervas came to Mallorca, well before January 1949. It seems probable that the first cursillo could only have emerged after the years of organizing the earlier "talks." Certainly at this point at San Honorato, the method was clearly judged as separate from Catholic Action. Yet this alone does not justify labeling this occasion the first cursillo. The problem is that the issue requires more explanation.

One part of the history remains with Bonnin. As a young college student involved with the young men's branch of Catholic Action and as a person who has lived cursillo for thirty years, this man holds the pieces, if not the key, to an answer. But he "does not feel that he enjoys the freedom to write the real history of the movement." As Rohloff mentions:

> The most valuable historical evidence has to be obtained from the archives of Eduoardo Bonnin, whose account of the history is not accepted by the National Cursillo Office of Spain.[3]

Like a well-known discovery of gold, many miners now claim the find as theirs. Yet acceptance of ownership is based on political allegiances, as much as evidence. Like a detective story halfread and half-ferreted out, the cursillo's history still remains to be completed. It seems that

Description of the Cursillo

the person who fashions the end controls the plot and the action of the characters.

But is there a hidden plot? Do the characters of Bonnin and Hervas, Juan Capo and Padre Segui stand for something other than themselves? What is at stake in deciding who is the real founder other than personal wins and losses for these men? One issue stands out among others. If Bonnin is considered the founder, then the cursillo is a lay movement begun by the laity and formed through their ideas and actions. For a highly clerical society, as Spain is, this becomes quite problematic. Given a Catholic hierarchy that wants and demands the organization and leadership of the church to be restricted to the domain of priests, there is a certain clerical edge in placing the first cursillo at the time of Capo and Hervas. It is a debate that was not resolved in 1949 and not in the years that followed. It still rages today, unsettled and disputed.

There is agreement that by January 7, 1949 both laity and clergy perceived the courses in a different light. By then the cursillo was the mark of something special: a method that could renew Catholic faith and change the lives of those who experienced the weekend. By this time, the cursillo as it is practiced today was established as a four-day weekend consisting of a series of courses dealing with the issues of Christ, community, and Christian love. As a method, its success in converting and revitalizing Christians was established.

Yet the courses were not without their failings. Although this method increased religious fervor and dedication, it could not sustain it. Enthusiasm and joy diminished in the months following an individual's participation in the courses. Something more was needed. For two years, the early Mallorcan group attacked the issue of perservance, yet one difficulty appeared to rest in the dis-

The Struggle to Exist

banding of priests and laity following initiation. Since individuals lived in different geographical areas and returned to separate parishes, there was no sustained interaction among initiates. Therefore, there was no basis for increasing the brotherhood and sisterhood, as well as the religious fervor fostered during initiation. Moreover, a strict regulation prohibited individuals from being initiated more than once, leaving few options for maintaining a commitment to the cursillo ideals.

In 1951, a solution was formulated. A follow-up program of weekly and bi-monthly meetings, called group reunions and *ultreyas,* regrouped initiates and thereby provided links of continuity. Once formulated, the meetings appeared to be an obvious solution, but they had resulted from two years of researching individuals from thirty-three initiations.

At this point, however, the history of the cursillo turns and twists again. Threads break and are rewoven. The political temper within the Spanish Catholic hierarchy led to changes in Mallorca. Given the cursillo's setting in Franco-dominated Spain, political aspects inevitably touched the cursillo. Franco, being somewhat connected with the approval of bishops and the affairs of the church, surreptitiously intervened in the situation in Mallorca. When Hervas became enmeshed in a disagreement with Bartolome Torres, a friend of Franco, it cost him his seat in Mallorca.[4] Soon afterwards, he was called to Cuidad Real and replaced by Jesus Enciso y Viana. It was not surprising that this new bishop opposed Hervas's ideas and was antagonistic to his method of renewal.

The cursillo was in trouble in its place of origin; it was banned and went underground. Through all of this, Bonnin continued to live the cursillo as did other Mallorcans,

Description of the Cursillo

but the impact of the method, being practiced secretly, was severely limited. The underground nature restricted the expansion of the cursillo in Mallorca.

Hervas left Mallorca, but he did not abandon the cursillo. The cursillo went with him; his forced removal strengthened his commitment to the movement. Now aligned by the Spanish hierarchy with the cursillo, Hervas had an interest in presenting this method as an unparalleled resource for the church. Hervas defended the cursillo as it spread to Cuidad Real and other areas of continental Spain.

The vision of the cursillo grew. The success of the cursillo in Cuidad Real led to the realization that it was not only a Mallorcan method but also possessed potential for revitalization throughout Spain. With its continued success, Hervas appraised its range as extensive as the church. He saw in it a method that could renew Catholicism as a whole and engender life to the old structure as well as aid in engineering the needed changes of the Spanish church.

The understanding of this perception resulted from many factors: the early years in Mallorca, the organization of the pilgrimage, the work of Bonnin, the influence of Franco's politics on the church, and the resultant apathy of churchgoers. It was here that Hervas contributed most to the growth of the cursillo. He became the public voice of the program; he became the public architect of Bonnin's and others' initial goals. Hervas was not the initial speaker, but his voice was an expansive echo. Through his role as bishop, Hervas provided the cursillo with the necessary national and, later, international exposure. He gave the "shove" which moved the cursillo from a parochial Mallorcan method to a world-ranging movement.

The Struggle to Exist

Hervas accomplished this transformation through the writing of texts. Since he was officially associated with the cursillo and identified as its leader by the Spanish Catholic hierarchy, he defended the very method he was aligned with. He began vindicating the cursillo by defining it and presenting information about its structure and its goals. It was as if Hervas accepted the hierarchy's definition that it was his movement and wrote from this perspective. That Hervas failed to mention the names of the early team members and especially the name of Edouardo Bonnin is significant. Their names as well as their ideas on the courses are absent from his text. Only Hervas's discontents and viewpoint mark the pages. The exclusion of the early Mallorcan team is an omission that leads outsiders to associate only one name with the cursillo: that of Juan Hervas. It is a position the clergy accepts and upholds.

In the process of writing texts, Hervas contributed not only to clarifying the method but also to its expansion. Through the texts, others are exposed to the new method and discover in it an aid in revitalizing their parishes. No one can say what the cursillo would have been without Hervas. It could have remained restricted to Mallorca. We do not know; it is only speculation. But we are certain of Hervas's actual influence and his significance. It marks the cursillo as definitively as Bonnin's ideas and conceptions do.

Clearly Hervas's effort in writing texts provided comprehensive documents that both defined the method and set limits to its misinterpretation. Prior to the texts, cursillo ideas were restricted to oral tradition. Later, goals and structures were written on mimeographed sheets that were forwarded to different diocesan areas. However, the mimeographed ideas contained original material interlaced with new ideas that represented both misinterpretations and assumed "improvements." Different diocesan groups incorporated ideas and projects they understood to be cursillo, yet with their various interpretations, many noncursillo aspects entered the method.

Hervas curtailed the fringe thoughts and "creative" changes by formulating definitive texts with an authorized interpretation. With the texts, the cursillo was directed toward a more uniform method that could remain intact during its expansion. Hervas specified the goals and set limits for the uses of these courses. Employing his texts, cursillo groups in Europe and America, in Africa and throughout the world, shaped their groups to the outline Hervas provided.

Looking back on the history of the cursillo, one leader, Bonnin, was underground in Mallorca, a place where he could not practice the very method he shaped, and a bishop was in Ciudad Real, now more tied to the method than Bonnin and publicly defending its plan of action. From these locations the cursillo expanded, yet it was Hervas's name that became associated with the cursillo as his texts accompanied the movement's expansion. The quiet, unassuming man living his life in Mallorca according to the principles he helped establish in the forties was hardly mentioned and ignored. In the following years, more and more is heard about Hervas, and less and less is heard about Edouardo Bonnin.

The drama of the cursillo embodies many actors, various scripts. Who do we believe? Who is the leading actor? It is safe to say that many of the original ideas were molded by Edouardo Bonnin, the ideas of environmental transformation, vibrant Christianity, and a living faith. He was the mainspring, the one who earnestly believed in this program and who fashioned the courses into the

The Struggle to Exist

cursillo. Hervas was the one who wrote the most about the plan and became the protector of the movement. Clearly both men were necessary for the movement to spread and succeed.

Like a quiet fire, fed and watched, Bonnin kindled this initial flame knowing it would produce heat for the years to come. Although Bonnin could not predict that this flame would become a sheet of fire, he glimpsed something else in the radiance that burned in Mallorca in the early forties. It was not his flame, but it was, in part, his bonfire. Once Hervas also sighted the light, he became the trusted nightguard of this flame; he assured that it would not go out, would not be doused with water. With the creative edge of Bonnin and the energetic, trusting protection of Hervas, the cursillo's expansion was guaranteed.

The first advance of the cursillo outside Spain occurred in 1951. From then on, the method traveled to other European countries, to Africa, and to the Americas. The number of members, now called cursillistas, increased as the method of renewal ranged across a wide geographical area. Six years later, the cursillo expanded to the United States, making its unlikely entrance at Lackland Air Force Base. The men who introduced the cursillo to the States were two Spanish Air Force cadets stationed in San Antonio. Bernado Vadell and Augustin Palomino brought the first cursillo to the States with the help of Fr. Gabriel Fernandez, T.O.R. On May 25, 1957, the cursillo took place in Waco, Texas, among Spanish-speaking people. It swept along the Southwest; San Angelo, Phoenix, Santa Fe, and Amarillo became active cursillo centers. From these regions cursillo leaders traveled to various dioceses introducing the program to areas such as Tucson; Lorain,

Description of the Cursillo

Ohio; Lansing, Michigan; and New York.

Although the cursillo influenced the cities of the East and West coasts, there was one definite limitation: the cursillos were presented in Spanish and thus prohibited English-speaking persons from joining. For this reason, the cursillo of November 9, 1961 is critical as it marks the first English version of the cursillo in the States. Fr. Fidelis Albrecht, O.F.M., offered an English version of the cursillo at the Mission of San Jose Church in San Angelo, Texas. Now, at last, the cursillo could become a serious force affecting American Catholicism.

At present, the ever-increasing number of initiations in the United States has produced an active group of proselytizers. The success of the cursillo here is reflected in the fact that no country exceeds the United States in the number of cursillo centers.

Because the scope of the cursillo is extensive, with an international membership of almost two million members, research on the movement necessitates definite geographic boundaries. Although members from midwestern and eastern dioceses have been interviewed, this study focuses on a specific center in Massachusetts that will be called Ocean Bay. This center generally recruits members from one diocesan area that includes Catholics from two major cities, each having a population of slightly over one hundred thousand, as well as individuals from the ten surrounding cities and towns. As a diocese, it has an unusually high percentage of national parishes, where priests and parishioners share the same ethnic background and conduct bilingual services. In these parishes frequently half of the Masses are said in English while the other half and other rituals such as the stations of the cross and baptism, use the language of the specific ethnic group. Most of the national parishes organize their own elementary schools with a focus on religion and ethnicity in basic educational curriculum. A few of the larger parishes maintain their own high schools, thereby establishing the religious and ethnic influences in the secondary socialization of their young parishioners. Increasingly these elementary and secondary schools, like many parochial schools in the United States, have suffered severe economic losses, forcing several to close. Yet, where possible, the national parishes in this diocese have tried to keep their schools open, even at significant costs to the parishes.

National churches, with bilingual services and structured educational formats, reinforce ethnic identity. At Ocean Bay, participation in the church is likewise an involvement in one's ethnic heritage. In fact, individuals in these parishes view themselves not only as Catholics but also as Portuguese Catholics, Polish Catholics, or French Catholics. In this way, ethnicity in this diocese is exceptionally important because it influences social action and shapes the identity of second-, third-, and fourth-generation immigrants. Since the majority of Catholics in this diocese belong to a national church, it is not surprising to discover many French, Portuguese, Polish, and Lebanese in the movement.

Ocean Bay has organized over ninety-four initiations since the center began in November 1964. Within this time, over thirty-five hundred people have been initiated. Since laity, priests, and religious brothers and sisters are eligible for membership, the following list provides a breakdown according to each category:

Laypersons	3,224
Priests	166
Religious Sisters	160
Religious Brothers	31

Description of the Cursillo

The occupations of members at Ocean Bay reveal a varied and extensive range including the semiskilled, the skilled, the clerical, the managerial, and the professional. There are carpenters, truck drivers, and machinists as well as lawyers, dentists, and surgeons. Yet even though all these individuals belong to the cursillo, there is a noticeable division within the movement. The white-collar workers, in particular the business executives, upper-level managers, and professionals tend to belong to the select group of leaders within the movement. Without doubt, they form, at Ocean Bay, the core within the core as they organize, guide, and direct the cursillo. This is not to say that blue-collar workers do not hold leadership positions; they do. But they are less apt to be selected, and when they are, it is after a longer period of active membership. Therefore, their leadership is noticeably less.

As a center, Ocean Bay consists of an active, committed group of members, strongly patterned according to the national directives for the movement. From its beginning in 1964, the center has followed the tenets of Hervas and has maintained close contact with the national organization of cursillos. As a center, it exhibits all phases of the cursillo, in its precursillo, initiation, and follow-up programs.

Ocean Bay offers the researcher a good opportunity for analyzing a center; it has been established for enough years to observe changes and to offer a perspective to gauge transformations. It is structured, carefully watched, and committed to strong leadership and to the cursillo as a way of life. Significantly, there has been continuity in directorship with one priest involved with its leadership since 1964. In many important ways, Ocean Bay provides a significant center to understand what cursillo is and to study it in action.

The Struggle to Exist

Examining the Ocean Bay Center affirms the position that the past lives in the present structure. That the cursillo evolved out of a plan for a pilgrimage accounts for its present triumphant character and the optimistic attitude of overcoming resistance. For members, the pilgrim notion is separate from any specific pilgrimage, as it bears witness to life as an ongoing journey. This also entails the notion of sacrifice, needed for carrying out the continual journey.

The direction of the Ocean Bay Center was set in motion in Mallorca in the seed of the early courses. The language at Ocean Bay is the language of its beginnings as the Spanish terms *de colores, palanca, ultreya, clausura,* and *rollo* are used by English-speaking members. Spanish words are voiced; they are not replaced by English substitutes. In this way, these words point back to its Mallorcan beginnings, as does the name cursillo de cristiandad.

The Spanish terms are reminders of its distinct beginning, involving the Mallorcan people of those early cursillo days. Yet familiarity with these Spanish terms and their easy incorporation with English words leads them to be anglicized and to be perceived as common words. It is as if the new terms, de colores, palanca, and ultreya, are, in a short time, not necessarily sensed as foreign. Even as these terms point back to Mallorca, they do so in a transient fashion.

Members at Ocean Bay, like members elsewhere, are aware that the cursillo began in Spain and that it is associated with the name Hervas, yet for many that is the extent of their information. Frequently their sense of its history consists of scattered pieces, that is, dates and some facts, which are at times incorrect. Asking members about the cursillo history reveals many vague and contradictory ideas. More accurate information is held by those who lead the cursillo because they are instructed on the early team in Mallorca, Hervas, and Bonnin. Yet even with the leaders, their range of historical perspectives is limited.

The name Bonnin is known at Ocean Bay as is his role in formulating a plan of renewal and as being an early leader. Yet Bonnin's name and significance would not be as well known if the Spiritual Director and some members had not, themselves, stopped by to visit Bonnin in Mallorca. Being impressed with the man, the Ocean Bay group invited Bonnin to spend ten days with them as they celebrated the tenth anniversary of the cursillo in their area. He accepted, and those who met him relate that "He is a beautiful, simple, humble, Christ-like man. He is very monklike. He eats simply, and he is like those in monasteries. He reminds me of Hook's picture of Christ."[5] Bonnin made a significant impression, and for members at Ocean Bay, Bonnin is not just a writer of the movement. He is seen as one of the founders by some, and as the founder by others. "Hervas was the protector of the cursillo, but not the originator. Bonnin is, yet he is not given credit." Exiled prophet, saint, shy, reticent man, which term fits Bonnin best is not certain, yet we can say that Bonnin is an integral figure in the history of the cursillo. Members contend that his full role awaits further disclosure.

If members know Bonnin the man, they also know Hervas the author. Hervas's documents are standard reading for members and leaders, including the *Cursillos in Christianity-Instrument of Christian Renewal, Questions and Problems Concerning Cursillos in Christianity,* and the *Leaders' Manual for Cursillos in Christianity.* These texts are the focus of extensive study and are the basis of knowledge for anyone actively involved in the movement. Because Hervas's words are read and studied, the cursillo at Ocean Bay shares a similarity with the cursillo at Mallorca and with those throughout the United States and other countries. In this sense, these documents successfully attain their objectives of adding consistency and standardization to the movement. Yet, to the extent that all texts are subject to various interpretations and a continual exegesis, it is a limited victory. Given that history, society, and culture transform textual material, the cursillo is continually subjected to forces that alter its structure and its style. This should be remembered in the examination of the Ocean Bay Center. This study is not an ethnography of "the" cursillo, but an analysis of one center that, although closely following the tenets and goals of Hervas and Bonnin, is not without its particular textual interpretations that have consequences for the organization and direction at Ocean Bay.

Description of the Cursillo

Notes

1. Geertz, "Religion as a Cultural System," in *Anthropological Approaches to the Study of Religion,* ed. M. Banton (NewYork: F. A. Praeger, 1966), p. 16.

2. M. Heidegger, *Poetry, Language, Thought,* trans. A. Hofstadter (New York: Harper and Row, 1975), p. 54.

3. I. Rohloff, *The Origins and Development of Cursillo* (Dallas: National Ultreya Publications, 1976), p. 4.

4. Ibid.

5. Any quotes without a specific footnote indicates the material is derived from interviews with members. References to all personal names are fictitious, to protect each individual's right to privacy.

CHAPTER 2

PREPARATION

AND TRAINING

FOR INITIATION

Description of the Cursillo

In spite of geography and history, Ocean Bay follows the early Mallorcan team in carrying out the three central phases of the movement. Phase one, or the precursillo, involves the issue of membership and recruitment, including the training of the team leaders structured to handle this process. Phase two focuses on initiation, the organized four-day rite of passage where the new members live cursillo. Then they move into the last phase, the follow-up, consisting of weekly and monthly gatherings to witness to the cursillo ideals.

Phase one is concerned with identifying, sponsoring, and recruiting new members. It is the phase of entrance into the movement, and success at this level means a constant flow of new members and the continual organization of initiations. Yet although the cursillo, like many movements, desires to attract new members, it does so with cautious restrictions. The goal is not new people *per se,* but new members where membership involves a paradigm of the acceptable individual. The cursillo does not want everyone, just the "right" people. Because of this, time is spent seeking out the ones who exemplify the ideals of the good member.

In this way, the cursillo insists on finding a selective group, namely, those possessing certain qualifications which make them ideal candidates. Requirements for candidates, then, are carved out of the image of the ideal member and are established to attract the right ones and, simultaneously, to turn away the others.

Some of the standard requirements for membership include:

1. *Age.* Individuals must be between the ages of twenty-five and fifty-five. It is claimed that this age group contains individuals who possess a certain maturity, yet who are not

Preparation and Training

too inflexible in their ideas. Persons over fifty-five are considered too entrenched in their conceptions of Catholicism, while those under twenty-five are labeled as too immature. In effect, the cursillo is an adult movement. That it discriminates against the young and the elderly is an outcome of its ideals. The age factor also means a predominance of married members. In the last few years, fewer single people have joined at Ocean Bay as the age criterion continued to rise. In some dioceses, the base is thirty, necessarily decreasing the chances that many single persons will be within this category. The change reflects the greater frequency with which single people abandon the movement when compared to the percentage of married couples who leave. Since the goal is active participation and not only attendance at initiation, the change in age attempts to attain this goal. Although the age restriction is strictly enforced, this does not preclude a few exceptions. For a person with prestige and power in a community, the fact that he or she is fifty-seven or fifty-eight may be waived, given other qualities. Also, some centers are more rigorous in enforcing the age restriction than others so that the number of exceptions varies from one location to another.

2. *Baptism.* The interested individual must be a Christian, baptized by a minister or priest. Non-Christians are not recruited, and neither

Description of the Cursillo

are they selected. The cursillo, in principle, is open to all Christians, but it is generally structured for Catholics. In the past, Protestants applied and were accepted at Ocean Bay, but since many did not continue the postcursillo activities, it has discouraged the present members from accepting many Protestants. However, it can be expected that in a diocese where the bishop and priests emphasize ecumenism, more non-Catholics will be selected. Clearly it is a Christian movement, geared to those familiar with and involved with Christianity. It begins with Christians and desires to change their lives. Thus the cursillo seeks out, from the beginning, practicing Christians and, more specifically, practicing Catholics.

3. *Mental and emotional stability.* Persons assessed as mentally unstable are not allowed to join. Since definitions of mental health are difficult to judge, this restriction is vague and not systematically enforced. If a person is receiving treatment in an out-patient clinic or has had a history of psychological problems, he or she would typically be refused candidacy. Where there are no public indicators of mental instability, private information and hearsay alleging emotional problems could warrant careful scrutiny to assess the presence of psychological problems. Members consider initiation a powerful mechanism that jolts candidates into a re-evaluation of their past lives; because of this,

Preparation and Training

initiation is considered too traumatic for certain individuals, causing added problems for the highly neurotic, not to mention the psychotic. In fact, there are individuals from Ocean Bay, as well as from other centers, who were institutionalized following their initiation. The stress of the cursillo weekend is realized, so that those who have problems in dealing with stress and change are prohibited. Yet, as stated, the category of mental stability is difficult to define and equally difficult to assure as a requirement for candidacy. Where cases of emotional instability are not discovered, these individuals are not precluded from joining.

Thus the cursillo is a movement in search of the emotionally healthy person. It avoids the problem case and seeks out the ordinary, relatively stable individual. The cursillo pursues those who feel they have no problems but who feel they are living only on the surface of their spiritual lives. It searches for the ordinary in order to create an extraordinary experience.

4. *Physical well-being.* Candidates must be in good health, with an absense of major physical problems. Although minor ailments and sicknesses are not deterrents, individuals with a past history of severe physical problems are discouraged from attending. The four days of initiation, with long hours and an exhaustive schedule of events, can create a strain. To prevent detrimental effects,

Description of the Cursillo

those with questionable health are discouraged, or in some cases, excluded from joining.

5. *Acceptable personality.* The cursillo searches for individuals who possess leadership qualities and who enjoy being with people. This category is especially ambiguous, but it does indicate a selectivity for certain types of individuals. The ideal member is a committed, dynamic, and powerful agent who is in a position of influence; in other words, one who can lead and energize others. Clearly the cursillo was not established for problem cases, and so individuals in the midst of personal problems are banned. Persons in the midst of marital problems and alcoholics are refused admittance. The cursillo avoids difficult cases, restricting membership to those who lack major emotional, physical, and situational problems.

6. *Mandatory initiations of husbands.* For married individuals, the husband's initiation must precede his wife's. If the husband refuses, his wife is excluded. His initiation is a necessary prerequisite for hers. This citerion stems from the Spanish beginnings of the cursillo and is related to the idea that women are more emotional and more religious than men. The wife's increased fervor may be problematic if it is not matched by some enthusiasm on the part of the husband. The requirement speaks to an idea of women cut from the Spanish cloth, yet at

times it coincides with the more traditional American definition of women.

Since the cursillo presents religion as a manly activity, this criterion pressures many men into joining, thereby increasing their numbers in the movement.

7. *Sponsor.* Unlike the previous six criteria, the last requirement does not pertain to any personal quality of the candidate athough it is still necessary for initiation. All interested individuals require a sponsor who is the link between the cursillo and themselves. This person supplies the candidate with an information sheet that must be completed and forwarded to the Board of Admissions, as well as being responsible for preparing the individual for initiation, with duties that continue into the postcursillo phase. Sponsors are encouraged to select individuals who conform to the cursillo requirements, so that sponsorship in itself provides for a certain selectivity.

   The sponsor must be an active member of the movement and one who has participated regularly in the follow-up activities for at least four months. This person must be willing to assume responsibility for the candidate's attendance at the weekly postcursillo meetings for a period of four months.

The requirements for candidacy illustrate the pursuit for a particular group of individuals. Since the cursillo contends that "the world is not lost because there are many pagans, but because there are few Christians who live and act as Christians,"[1] it selects men and women who are predisposed to becoming more Christian. It neither looks to the very young nor to the very old, but to the middle range. Likewise, it searches out neither the alcoholic nor the criminal, but the well-respected citizen. The cursillo is not so much concerned with having a large membership as it is with acquiring an *active* membership. Its aim is to have a core of Christians who are vibrant, enthusiastic, and committed.

One recurrent image used to describe this ideal group is that of a well-trained military unit. The language of the cursillo is marked with military analogies and references that signal a prepared group ready to act when called. It implies a hierarchical structure with a chain of command and the growth of a militant Christianity where the mission is: "(a) to look for militants; (b) to choose them; (c) to welcome them; (d) to train them; (e) to make use of them."[2] But if the cursillo is militant, it is the militancy of the early church marked by courage and fight. It is an atmosphere characterized by zeal, confidence, and commitment. Granted the target has changed, for the main concern is no longer the "pagans" who hindered the spread of the early church. Neither is the target outsiders or nonbelievers, but the members of the church itself—the baptized men and women who no longer practice their religion, as well as those who participate lifelessly and without passion in church rituals.

Thus, a significant clue in understanding the cursillo is that its target is within the church and at times the church itself. The cursillo is opposed to religion performed out of fear or duty; it preaches a religion of love and passion. It is a method that differs from the traditional Catholic approach and involves an attack on the

Preparation and Training

very language and programs assessed as unsuccessful in Catholicism.

Thus, the analogy of a militant, Christian group signals the mobilization of individuals (cursillo membership), the preparation and training (initiation and the Leaders' School), a plan of attack (cursillo methodology), and a series of tactics (postcursillo activities). The target is the lifeless religion of traditional Catholicism. It is in this sense that the cursillo endeavors to create a corps which is *engagé*, and it selects its members with this goal in mind. Yet the condition of being *engagé* does not necessarily encourage social action, for it is not so much a physical condition as a spiritual state, that is, a particular state of mind. For the cursillo, it is a state of spirituality.

This elite, however, is an ideal of the cursillo and, as such, is not always realized. There have been, and there will continue to be, times when the candidates for initiation do not measure up to the ideals of leadership. The actualization of this goal will depend on the number of people willing to join and the degree to which requirements for candidacy are enforced.

An organization exists to ascertain that the right individuals are selected, for it is felt that incorrect decisions in the precursillo stage are detrimental to both the success of initiation and the follow-up program. To speak of the precursillo phase then is to speak, at least indirectly, of the secretariat, which is the basic regional structure, primarily established to direct the movement. Its mission is to oversee the operation of the movement within the diocese, with a concern for each phase of the cursillo. The body entrusted to accomplish this goal is led by the spiritual director. He is the voice of the cursillo in a particular episcopal area, and it is his responsibility to guide and strengthen the movement. At Ocean Bay, the spiritual director is a priest who was appointed in 1965 and, as previously mentioned, has continued in this role for the last fourteen years, providing continuity to the cursillo program in this area. The spiritual director is not the only member of the secretariat; he works in conjunction with a five-member group, predominantly laity, composed of a president, a secretary, a treasurer, a representative of men, and of women.

The secretariat, in order to assure qualified candidates, sets up a special board that evaluates the applications of sponsored inidividuals. The board of admissions, composed of a rector, a rectora, and one of the assistant spiritual directors who is a priest, receives the potential candidate's information sheet and assesses whether requirements are met. Cases of physical illness, divorce, and borderline situations are evaluated by this group, whose decisions are also influenced by the additional information provided by the sponsor's sheet. Questions such as "Are there any noteworthy health or medical precedents in his or her family?" and "Has (s)he ever suffered from a severe nervous condition?" are asked about the candidate. The sponsor as well must answer to the following, "Do you assume the responsibility of getting your candidate to the Cursillo? Sending Palanca? Attending the Closing? Taking your candidate home? Offering assistance to the family at home?"

Even if a person meets all the requirements, he or she may not be initiated immediately, since each initiation has additional stipulations that limit the number of persons from certain particular categories. No more than five candidates from one parish, nor more than three religious brothers and one religious sister per order, are admitted at each initiation. In addition, seminarians and students are disallowed. These specifications for each in-

Preparation and Training

itiation can at least postpone one's initiation. For example, there have been some women, mostly religious, who at one time waited over a year to attend.

The secretariat has a responsibility that extends beyond the selection of candidates, for it both organizes and trains a select group from which future team leaders will, in part, be singled out. The secretariat is charged with the organization of the Leaders' School, which is more recently called Workshops in Christian Living. Initiation is related to the existence of the Leaders' School because the school is instituted to train the members who will organize the four-day program—the men or women who will give the doctrinal presentations, called *rollos*, and participate in planned activities for the candidates. These "talks" are central to the initiation since they form the doctrinal basis of the movement, and as such, they require preparation, theological knowledge, and a forceful presentational style. A purpose of the Leaders' School is to accomplish this systematically and successfully.

The members of the Workshops in Christian Living gather weekly, conducting their meeting according to a set format. The meeting is so highly structured that each section has a specific time allotment. The general format is as follows:

Structure

Prayer to the Holy Spirit
Group Reunion
Doctrinal Lecture
Class in Techniques
Sections
Examination of Conscience
Visit to the Blessed
Sacrament

Description of the Cursillo

The workshops, as a structure, illustrate Hervas's tenet that "in the cursillo nothing is trusted to improvisation."

The opening prayer, the group reunion, and the closing actions are not exclusive to the Leaders' School for they occur as part of each member's weekly meeting. The remaining three segments, however, are restricted to the Leaders' School as they comprise the methods of preparing men and women to be efficient instructors. The doctrinal lectures, given by a priest, focus on theological and spiritual issues, and are divided into two categories: the first emphasizes doctrinal areas specific to the cursillo, and the second is directed to general areas of Christian dogma. The number of meetings spent on one subdivision is arbitrary, and may depend on the special interest and training of the priest, the personal direction of the spiritual director, or even the accidental visit of a well-respected priest to the area.

The technique section entails a twenty-five minute talk by a lay person. Methodology is the focus, with explanations offered on the psychological aspects of various techniques and the rational of certain cursillo procedures. Here individuals come to understand the interworkings of the cursillo as the method is dissected, examined, and explained.

The sections are groups specializing in one of six areas of the organizational structure of the movement. These research and work groups collect, organize, and distribute information on the cursillo. Some sections, such as the general one, keep check on the number of initiations planned in the area and in neighboring dioceses as well as examining the actual and potential weaknesses of the cursillo. The precursillo section, meanwhile, constructs the personal information sheets of the candidates, handles transportation of candidates, and arranges the housing of initiates. In this way, the work of the section aids in

Preparation and Training

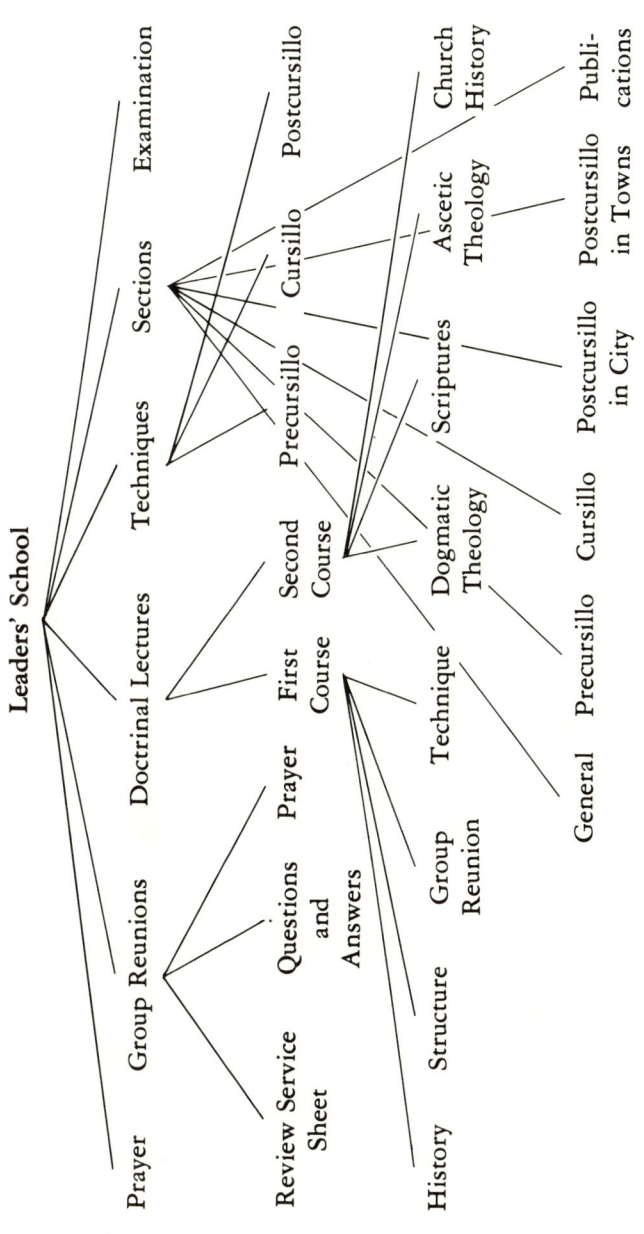

carrying out the bureaucratic duties of the diocesan secretariat.

The Leaders' School, as evident in figure 1, provides training and knowledge through the study of church dogma and the examination of the cursillo method. Yet it is not only a school, but also a Christain environment shaped by these members. It is both the place where one obtains information about the cursillo and the context in which one applies its ideals and beliefs. One learns about the cursillo community while being a part of this social unit.

At this point, it is important to ask, How do members plan for an initiation? What is entailed in creating a rite of passage? When an initiation is scheduled, it is mostly from the Leaders' School that a team is selected. Of the ten lay persons, generally half are experienced organizers of past initiations, while the other five are novices. The Director will try to make certain that these ten represent different parishes and various age groups.

The first task is the formation of a team that will coordinate and direct the four-day initiation. However, the team is not just a group whose function is to oversee the program of initiation. The team must not only *do;* they must also *be* a living, Christian witness to the cursillo ideals. They are not just part of it; they must also live it. In this way, the preparation for initiation engenders an atmosphere marked by Christian ideals and the formation of a closely linked group.

The team must not only be prepared to preach; they must also guide through their speech. Thus their talks, called rollos, are not words about religion, but words alive with their experience. The talk is a "witness," an experience shared, with team members expected to speak not through a mask or to hide behind rhetoric. It is from the heart that their words are ideally expected to come. The rollo must be their story, as well as being a talk with a specific cursillo focus. It is their testimony to the candidates, individuals they are united with as spiritual searchers and, hopefully, as future cursillo followers. The one difference is that the team members have discovered a spiritual presence; religion is a force in their lives.

Thus the team members speak from experience. Yet it is not a "telling" of this experience but, as Heidegger would distinguish, a "showing." Thus their aim is to teach, where teaching is conceptualized as an offering, a giving to another of one's spiritual insights. "You share yourself. You must be authentic. You can't witness to what you are not." These words from a rectora sum up the expected direction of the talks. The goal is as simple as teaching and, as anyone who teaches knows, as difficult, wrought with hazards and possible disappointments. Aware of the possibility of failure, the team prepares, anticipating the amount of time and the number of meetings needed for a successful venture.

How do these ten members become a team? After a date for the initiation is selected by the spiritual director and the former rectora, a new rectora or rector is chosen, depending on whether it is a women's cursillo or a men's, for one of the rules of initiation is the separation of the sexes. If it is a rectora, she then begins with a period of prayer, performed and offered for the formation of the team. The first person chosen is the most unusual member: the palanca lady. Of all the team, her role is specifically as a praying member, and once this person accepts, the remaining individuals can be selected.

There is but one central goal for the team—to bring about *metanoia* in the candidates. The aim is a dramatic change in the candidates and the structuring of a ritual

Description of the Cursillo

that can inaugurate this dramatic molding of the "new person." The group's intention, then, is the consolidation of a four-day weekend that will be a powerful rite of passage for the candidates. Committed to this aim, the group struggles to create a working team.

This objective necessitates critical thinking about each part of the weekend and, for many, the information acquired in the Workshops of Christian Learning. The team will come together as an embodiment of the Christian community; therfore love, care, and unselfish giving ideally mark the organization of the initiation. The goal requires time and personal energy from the team. Yet, since this is judged a paramount event, time is found for the months of preparation necessary for the organization of the weekend.

First, a great effort is made to single out a group of individuals who are well suited to the task; this demands that the rectora, the spiritual director, and the palanca lady pay careful attention to the capacities, accomplishments, and flair of potential leaders. Once each person is chosen, the next step consists in instilling a sense of unity. If this group is to lead the weekend, it must exhibit the characteristics of a team: caring, commitment, cooperation, and spirit. To reach this unity, a series of meetings are established in order that the group may form a fellowship before the destined weekend.

The first meeting occurs at the home of the rectora. Here each person presents a brief personal history; the rectora listens for clues that might help in deciding which woman is best suited for each talk. It is hoped that the match between talk and person may be a good one, for the success of the cursillo starts at this stage. After the meeting, the rectora and the palanca lady pray that the decisions may be auspicious.

Preparation and Training

The second meeting takes place at the location of the future cursillo weekend. Here the assistant spiritual director discloses the purpose of each of the talks and conveys their essential meaning for the weekend. Each person is assigned a tablemate, who is another team member, to sit with at one of the five tables during initiation. In addition, individuals are informed of their particular assignment, namely, one of the fifteen rollos. It is up to each member to research and think through the specific topic, making certain, however, that she complies with the directives of the leaders' manual. Because each rollo has a definite purpose with a certain style and tone intended, members must conform to the manual while also contributing a testimony from their experiences. They must merge the unique with the general in a balance not easily achieved. The rollo provides an opportunity to present knowledge of cursillo dogma while simultaneously witnessing to its effect on one's life. It is for this reason that rollos demand research and study and are a time-consuming project. There is Mass, and then they discover they have four weeks to compose their talk.

From this time on, there will be communication between team members, as they keep in contact, sharing their difficulties and their fears. Individuals will pray for each other and aid members who are especially frightened by the task ahead. For some, it is an enormous step marked by doubts, hesitation, and nervousness. Yet the sharing of feelings is encouraged, and the atmosphere created is of a supportive and uplifting group. They are being prayed for, thought about, and they know that others care. During this period, they write letters to each other, telephone, and visit each other when possible.

Because belonging to the team requires much time, attention is given to the team's family, especially the spouse. Therefore, the spouse is invited to some meetings, and the evening becomes a social event as well as a working session. Generally food is brought, and the potluck supper provides a night of socializing for the couple, not just an evening away from home for the team member. This is the format for the third gathering. By this meeting, the team members' talks are completed, and three copies are given to the rectora. As one member expressed it, "There is a sense of community building. One senses the bonds. There is a deep love and a sense of oneness. We start to think about and pray for those "coming in." For many members, the team spirit is felt and experienced by this time. The community takes shape and the qualities expected of this alliance start to be manifested. Also, at this point, the group begins to focus on those candidates who will be coming in, the new members, who will soon join the larger community. The sense of purpose is felt, and the team becomes a real force in their lives.

Two weeks later, at a business meeting, the talks of the members are handed back with suggestions. There may be too much witnessing or not enough, or members may be asked to stress points they overlooked. The talk must fulfill two purposes: it must be a witness by the individual and a message about a specific topic essential to the weekend. Initiation centers around fifteen talks, each one thought-out not only by the secretariat but also years back in the work of the early Mallorcan team. It is the ideas of Bonnin and Hervas that they must witness to. Thus the aim of each presentation is a fusion of cursillo ideals with the interpretation of speciic spiritual ideas, the meshing of the established topic and a unique expression, the fusing of objective ideals and a personal witness. In this way, writing a rollo is not unlike being asked to write an essay

Preparation and Training

on an assigned topic, following the expected literary rules, and being expected to clearly mark the text with personal experience.

Two days later, a day of recollection occurs. It will be a night of socializing and of praying, to unify the group for the last time before the forthcoming cursillo. The following weekend will be the weekend of initiation; for many members this experience will be as intense as their own initiation. Some will echo this man's expression:

> It was more powerful than initiation. Living cursillo was a conversion. But this was the cream, the frosting on the cake. I developed a relationship with the team. I was brought closer to Truth, to God. Ten guys getting together, two spiritual directors, one rector.
> There was a sense of being called to bring others because God is calling them. It had to be. There was a honing oneself down. There was a sense of responsibility for these men, and one owed it to these guys. There was letter writing and praying for each other. There was a bond with the table mate. It was supportive; we prayed together. There was a friendship through the team, and they are still maintained.

This is the weekend they have been preparing for and struggling to organize. It is the time for action and a time of action.

Although the team anticipates the candidates, it cannot be said that the candidate is ready for the team. The team member arrives with full knowledge of what is to come, while the candidate comes with minimum information, if any at all.

Description of the Cursillo

The candidates are unaware of the efforts and time devoted by the team. They do not know of this group's existence, nor do candidates realize that some of the individuals sitting at their tables are not candidates like themselves, but team members camouflaging their identities. Also they are unaware of the existence of the secretariat or the formation of the Leaders' School. The candidates, then, arrive for the weekend limited in their information. This is planned, for secrecy is essential to the cursillo.

Several years ago the secrecy at Ocean Bay was very strictly enforced. Few divulged any information about initiation to a nonmember even if this outsider was their spouse, friend, or relative. When, in the early seventies, individuals were questioned about the cursillo, they frequently refused answers; members generally avoided discussing any specifics about the initiation or the follow-up meetings. They admitted their membership in the movement and their enthusiasm for its techniques, but skirted conversations dealing directly with the structure of the cursillo. Many viewed secrecy as a binding vow whether ot not it was so intended, refusing to divulge any particulars. The following two quotations illustrate this tenet of secrecy upheld by many at Ocean Bay during this time:

> If you make a cursillo, come and see me, and I will tell you all my experiences with the cursillo. But until then, I won't say anything.

> I would hate to break the secrecy. It was a personal experience. If the rules have been changed, then I could and would tell you about my experiences, but if the rules haven't changed, then I can't say anything. Until you make one, then I can't say anything about the cursillo.

Preparation and Training

Although secrecy was intended to maintain surprise and bolster the impact of initiation, it became something more—a vow ritualistically kept, producing an aura of a secret brotherhood and sisterhood. At times, desirable candidates rejected the cursillo because of their skepticism for secrecy, conceiving of this code as a childish game. Due to the substantial negative reaction by both members and nonmembers, the position concerning secrecy has altered.

At Ocean Bay, candidates are now issued a leaflet with questions and answers on the cursillo as well as a sheet entitled, "What You Should Know When You Make a Cursillo." Individuals, in contrast to several years back, are told to expect fifteen talks and discussions in an environment of warmth and sharing. They hear that the "cursillo deals primarily with fundamentals of Christianity" and that there is "nothing very novel about a cursillo." Meetings are scheduled before initiation to dispel misgivings or uncertainties. Here they glimpse a general orientation to initiation, and their questions about the cursillo are answered. Even though more information is presently provided, there is much that remains hidden. For example, to reveal there are fifteen talks reaffirms the idea that the cursillo is similar to a Catholic retreat rather than establishing a contrasting perspective on the cursillo, a position that is not necessarily discouraged.

Members today generally concur with the newer stand of reduced secrecy and relative openness. This position exists even among individuals who, when interviewed five years ago, had refused to divulge any information. Many now consider total secrecy as unnecessary, if not foolish. Consider the present position of one of the leaders at Ocean Bay, a man who had strongly upheld the secrecy code in the early seventies:

Description of the Cursillo

> Awhile back, the secrecy code was strictly enforced. People would foolishly refuse to disclose any information on the cursillo. This is silly and stupid. You can tell people there are fifteen talks, etc. Since the cursillo involves a personal response, everyone's reaction is different, and it can't be programmed.

The change in attitude toward secrecy is not the result solely of the skepticism and distrust experienced at Ocean Bay, but a general discontent in many regions. In effect, the breaking of the secrecy code results from a policy change on a national scale, instigated by the national secretariat. This board informs the regional branches of alterations in policy, and serves to disseminate information on new orientations and procedures. The national secretariat assures that Hervas's method and doctrine will continue with a degree of consistency by providing guidelines and recommendations. To accomplish its supervisory functions, it has a director, secretary, and treasurer, and from its headquarters in Texas, it publishes a national magazine that disseminates new ideas. To further accomplish its coordinating task, the national secretariat organizes yearly national conventions that draft platforms to air problems in the cursillo methodology and structure. The secrecy code, then, is one example where modifications in national policy affect the attitude and behavior of regional groups. In this way, the shifts in the rules of secrecy illustrate the interrelationship of the cursillo center at Ocean Bay with the larger national secretariat.

However, even with a greater openness, initiates are basically uninformed about the cursillo. They may know there are fifteen talks and that the focus is on Christian living, but their understanding remains vague. As one man acknowledged, "I had no idea what it was. I thought

Preparation and Training

it was a four-day retreat with a fancy name." So some go anticipating a relaxed weekend while others attend with reservations ranging from hesitation and ambivalence to distrust. Why, then, do individuals go? What factors lead them to give up one day's work, sacrificing their leisure time and the cost for room and board? One factor lies in the requirement that husbands must be initiated before their wives. Because of this stipulation, many men attend the cursillo so their wives may be initiated: "My wife wanted to go on a cursillo. She asked me to go, and I went." Other men need more coaxing by their wives; but, in time, they decide to attend.

The persistent voice is not always the wife's. Members constantly attempt to get others to join, and friends and relatives become targets for proselytizing. Frequently, tired of being asked, the friend decides to attend.

> I joined because I was forced to do so to get the guys off my back. I had the form (information sheet) for applying for one year and didn't use it till then.

Initiation becomes, for many, the best among several negative options, as this woman explains her husband's decision:

> A pediatrician Paul Hodge had made it. He was "flying"—shaking as he spoke of the cursillo—yet unwilling to disclose any information. He kept nagging my husband and some other men to make a cursillo. He wouldn't stop nagging, and they finally got so fed up they went to shut him up.
>
> My husband went with a terrible attitude. He felt he was wasting his time but felt it was worth going just to get him off his back.

Description of the Cursillo

Just as some attend to relieve social pressures, many are enticed by the little they have heard, namely, the joy of the weekend and the euphoric feelings revealed by other initiates. The enthusiasm and perserverance of friends and family frequently contribute to an individual's decision to attend. Members, overjoyed with their own initiation, prod, nag, and coax their friends into going. Convinced it will be a wonderful experience, they greet friends with, "You'll love it; you should make it," and "Have you thought of going?" Curious or enthused, certain individuals take up the offer and become initiated.

When the elated initiate is one's spouse, many wives look forward to the forth-coming weekend. A significant percentage of the wives at Ocean Bay cite the desire to share the cursillo experience with their husbands as their reason for attending. They wish to be included in the experience which produced such profound effects on their partners.

> My husband came in at one o'clock in the morning. I had waited up for him. He didn't want to spoil it for me, so there were some things he didn't say. But he did share in some of the moments, and I felt excited about going. Because I wanted to share this experience with him, I couldn't wait to attend.

Some wives want to share their husband's experiences but not if it means spending a weekend with forty other women. When they go, they leave reluctantly.

> If one of the couple has made one, they like the other to make one. But I put it off. I didn't have the enthusiasm Malcolm had. Finally I said, let me get it over with. That was my attitude.

Preparation and Training

There are some husbands, however, who do not just ask their wives to be initiated; they demand that it be shared, leaving the women with few options.

> I signed up my wife and told her to fill in the papers (information sheet) since she was going anyway. She had no choice. I don't usually push, but I wanted to share this.

His wife agreed she had no choice, for when he returned from initiation on Sunday night, he was ready to pack her bags. Since he was so adamant, she went.

As frequently happens, the weekend may also be "given" by a member to an individual who is wavering. In this situation, the person is sponsored and the costs are paid by the sponsor. Many cannot easily refuse such a gift.

> They asked me regularly if I would go. Then the straw, the last one, was a Christmas gift of a woman to me. She had booked me for the January one.

Likewise a woman reported that her husband had been given the cursillo weekend by a parish priest who was also a close friend. The priest then said, "After your husband goes, you'll go." For some, it is the gift they cannot refuse. If they could disregard the question, "When will you go?" many cannot decline the invitation as a present. People are affected by this generosity as one man was, who recalled with emotion how he had been offered the weekend by a priest. Deeply touched, he went.

To be sure, there are some individuals who are searching, sensing problems in their lives. This applies particularly to those Catholics caught between the pre-Vatican II ideas and the post-Vatican reform. Unable to make sense

Description of the Cursillo

of the changes in Catholicism or of where they are headed spiritually, they approach the cursillo as a possible answer.

> I had heard about it. Sounded like something I'd like to try. Felt it was a new outlook on Catholicism. I was a catechism product.

Information on the cursillo leads them to attend with the hope of finding a ready-made solution.

> I was searching for something. I was looking. I had seen the cursillo "advertised" in a bulletin. Later, I attended a meeting, and Rupert slipped me an application. It seemed exciting, different, and something I'd enjoy.

Some are troubled with the general problems of living, with the everyday burdens of existence and do not feel up to what they must handle. They see in cursillo a solution to their problems, a possible avenue in time of need.

> I was having problems. I was searching for something. My son was giving us some problems. He was stoned and smoking so much that he couldn't stand up and popping pills and alcohol. I didn't know what to do, and it was upsetting, and I was crying, and then I started to pray. I was searching for something, and it changed my life.

Although the cursillo does not desire attracting individuals with problems, be they marital, family, alcohol, or drugs, some with these personal difficulties do find their way into the cursillo. It is hard to establish whether someone is coping or not, when his or her troubles are serious or just part of the minor challenges of daily living. Also,

Preparation and Training

as long as personal and family problems remain hidden and there is no public stigma, such as time in a mental institution, drug rehabilitation, membership in Alcholics Anonymous, or some other acknowledged problem, candidates will be admitted.

Then there are some who attend because clients and employers pressure them at work to attend. Some public officials and teachers in Catholic schools feel the necessity to attend. Also, this applies to some parish priests who think the weekend will be beneficial, letting them know what is happening to their parishioners. They consider cursillo involvement profitable in their roles as priests and embark on the weekend to discover what this phenomenon entails. This was especially applicable in the early seventies when cursillo at Ocean Bay was misunderstood. Presently it is more established, safer, and more integrated into the work of the diocese. Certainly not all priests are intiated for this reason:

> While I was at the seminary, I had contact with cursillistas and found most of them to be bright, involved, and all you wanted them to be. They were also realistic.
>
> I had been the recipient of their good work and wanted to say thanks to them and show my apprciation to them, the cursillo community.

In speaking to members, what is evident is the range of motivations for their attending a cursillo. Yet given the stipulation requiring husbands to be initiated before their wives, there develops a pattern whereby many men attend mainly to allow their wives the opportunity of becoming members. To those who study movements, this is especially important, since often the literature on movements emphasizes crises situations as an explanation for recruitment, pointing to members' psychological problems. Although these factors apply to some in the cursillo, there are a significant number of individuals who are initiated, not because they are in the midst of a crisis, but because of a requirement, without which they would never have joined. Obviously the motivations for their remaining are not the same as the reasons which led them to attend. But it is important to consider the range of factors involved in people's decisions to join movements.

Given this requirement, a significant number of married men leave for the weekend skeptical, or at least ambivalent. They go not envisioning great changes. Yet, whatever their expectations, the weekend generally turns out to be quite different than anticipated. What they could not predict is the actual experience and their response. Some never return the same.

Notes

1. J. Hervas, *Cursillos in Christianity—Instrument of Christian Renewal,* trans. W. Young (Phoenix: Ultreya Press, 1965), p. 62.

2. Ibid., p. 382.

CHAPTER 3

LIVING

CURSILLO

Description of the Cursillo

Enthused or hesitant, optimistic or somewhat dejected—in whatever mood, the candidates arrive Thursday to begin their initiation, where they will remain until Sunday evening. What will fill the space and time in this period is the question they all face. What they experience is the answer.

The Thursday structure is extremely interesting both in format and in its meaning since it follows the lines of a traditional Catholic retreat. The tone is somber, and the atmosphere meditative as individuals examine their past lives. The themes of this night are helplessness, loneliness, and salvation through self-denial and self-surrender which are pointedly expressed in the three meditations preached that evening.

The first meditation, entitled "Know Yourself," is aimed at the individuals' past actions. Its purpose is to direct the candidates to reflect on their mental and spiritual states. The question, Why have you come to the cursillo? is raised, and they are made aware that the answer is to know yourself and to discover what you are really like. It is here, in this very first talk, that the candidates are informed of the importance of reflection.

> The evil of our days, the great malady that afflicts the man of today is the lack of meditation, the lack of time and tranquility. We live on impressions. We do not find ourselves; we do not know ourselves. We lose our identity . . . life, business, pleasures crush us.[1]

Individuals understand that they have the ability to change and to question. Human beings are portrayed as dynamic, active agents who, because of their ability to think, to formulate, and to dream can alter their lives and their world.

> However, you are not just an object. You are a man . . . a rational being. You cannot renounce your faculty of reasoning. You must organize your life; bring order into your affairs so that you may be free; so that you will not live enchained, enslaved, disillusioned, frustrated.[2]

They are encouraged to look themselves squarely in the face—a task which they alone must initiate. They are directed to focus on their personal selves in order that reflection may lead to a restructuring of their lives.

The purpose of the first meditation is to foster awareness by directing the individuals to reflect on their past actions and their previous social relationships. It calls into question the generally unreflective nature of their lives and encourages the initiates to confront themselves.

> WHAT ARE YOU REALLY LIKE? Do you want to be convinced that you are not as good as the world thinks you are? Think for a moment.
>
> Would you like to have the true story of your life filmed? Would you be able to view all your actions, your ambitions, your pretenses, your conversations, on the screen without blushing? Would you want your friends to be present at the showing? Would you want your children, your mother, your wife, your sweetheart to know it? Don't worry. They will not see it. No official censors will review it. But the Lord has seen it. And you, too, must see it in these moments of sincerity . . . .[3]

The message of the second meditation echoes the first. This is not accidental, but is consciously programmed; all meditations are purposefully designed to reinforce the objectives of initiation. In this way, the style, the format, and the tone are intertwined to attain the desired changes in the initiates. Because of this, there are explicit demands on the team to maintain the programmed order and unity in all talks in order to harness the most significant impact. As they divulge:

> To jolt and awaken the conscience was the objective of the previous meditation (Know Yourself); in this one (The Prodigal Son) *we must take a further step.* We must make the cursillista feel, almost without his being aware of it, *the torture of his conscience and the need for forgiveness,* in order to throw himself, as the total solution, on the mercy of Christ's heart, which is to constitute the marrow of this meditation.[4]

The second meditation, "The Prodigal Son," also directs the individuals back to their past as it encourages the candidates to examine, in greater detail and degree, their imperfections and failures. They are driven to confront the serious problems in their lives and to juxtapose the ideal life with their present pattern. They apprehend that, like the prodigal son, each person can receive forgiveness; however, it demands the admission of guilt and repentance.

The last meditation on Thursday is entitled "The Three Glances of Christ." Again the theme of sinful existence is intoned as the candidates are offered a glimpse of salvation through repentance. This tone is emphasized by the team members who understand that:

> After the meditation on the Prodigal Son, the cursillista has been left with a clear vision of his wretchedness before Christ's mercy. His reaction

and its consequences must now be oriented by citing to him some typical examples of various reactions in the face of the Lord's goodness.[5]

Clearly, Thursday is structured to effect a disorientation of the candidates, that is, to plunge them into a shocking state of self-awakening. The individuals must handle this shock in isolation since they are prohibited from speaking with other candidates and must maintain silence. They are segregated from others and left without any supportive group to share their frustrations and anxieties. Candidates listen to words that may upset them and that are designed to do exactly this. The images and examples are purposefully selected to instil aloneness and helplessness.

It is not surprising that certain individuals experience a break with their past lives that very night. Although most individuals experience a shock Friday or Saturday, there are some drastically affected by the events of the first night. As one Spanish man reports:

> You saw yourself as being so small, so wretched, so completely insignificant, that you began to live the words, "I will arise; I will go to my father!" You felt sure that if on your side you did what poor human possibilities permit, the father of the prodigal son would open his arms to you in the sacrament of repentance. That evening I made up my mind to confess my sins.[6]

Yes, some are "struck" that first night. The atmosphere of critical reflection and of meditation imparts an immediate, powerful stimuli.

> Thursday night made the Stations of the Cross relevant. They had always been abstract, and I

could never sink my teeth in it. Before the cursillo, I didn't see myself as religious; I saw myself as hypocritical. Then the Prodigal Son had an impact. It gave me permission to have been inadequate, to start anew. I was off and running.

One factor which marks the first evening, as well as the entire initiation, is the sense of unpredictability. The candidates find themselves in an unfamiliar setting with few clues as to what to expect. They cannot easily prepare themselves to react since they are unaware of what is to come. The tenet of secrecy, even when modified, assures that they will be uninformed and possessing few ways to guard against the forthcoming events. Many, then, will be unprepared for handling the unexpected.

Individuals, however, are not left entirely without indicators. The first night does provide a definition of the situation since it is instituted as a traditional Catholic retreat. The candidate is led to assume that initiation will proceed in a manner similar to a retreat. Silence and an instrospective attitude reinforce this position. Yet, just as the individual becomes accustomed to silence and meditation, this orientation, like a wind change, shifts.

The following morning, the somber and individually centered format is punctured by a tone of happiness and an atmosphere of shared fellowship. Each person now surprisingly gathers that social interaction, discussions, and a joyful spirit are vital. Unprepared for this transition, many are startled and confused:

> I came out of Mass in a deeply meditative state of mind. The same attitude could be observed among the others. *Then the silence which had been reigning since the previous evening was broken by a song which is very popular in Spain*

> ... I did not like that. I was not in the habit of singing at the top of my voice on coming out of church. Then the members of the directing team began to laugh and joke. One could see that they were sincerely happy and joyful, but their laughter seemed to me out of place after the deeply serious moments we had just experienced in chapel.
>
> In this way, talking, singing, and joking, we then made our way towards the dining room. I noticed that, like myself, many people found the overflowing joy of the directing team out of place.[7]

Since the remaining days are marked by joy and social interaction, we may ask why the Thursday night format is included. Members at Ocean Bay remark that this format leads individuals to "take it seriously" so that candidates will not "waste time." The movement generally recruits Catholics, and since many have attended retreats, they readily consider the cursillo another retreat. Asked to be silent and required to listen to solemn talks, they are inclined to take this initiation seriously sensing in this ritual, what Mead points to as the "extra degree of intensity."[8] Because of their past experiences, they appraise these four days as a critical time. It is not a vacation nor an interval for physical labor nor for instruction, but days similar to others spent on a religious weekend. The silence, the somberness, and the introspection are expected because candidates align the cursillo with a retreat, providing an interpretive structure for understanding this evening and disposing them for the forthcoming days.

For this reason, negating the retreat framework confuses the candidates who expect continuity between

Description of the Cursillo

Thursday and Friday. Yet this jolt establishes a clear demarcation, contrasting the older traditional approach and the newer cursillo structure. In fact, the cursillo proper begins after Mass on Friday morning when joy and enthusiasm replace the retreat format and its somber attitude. Although Friday is the second day for the initiates, it is addressed in the movement as the first day. On this day, and not Thursday, the cursillo officially dawns.

The retreat format provides a point of contrast between the cursillo and traditional Catholic methods, yet the structure has a further purpose. Not only does it emphasize the distinction between a retreat and the cursillo, it makes the difference an acceptable one. The cursillo remains aligned with traditional Catholicism by being couched in the shadow of an authorized Catholic experience. In this way, the retreat validates initiation by being juxtaposed to it and by employing certain retreat-like procedures throughout the weekend, such as: (*a*) the role of some priests as preachers, (*b*) the intoning of traditional Catholic prayers, (*c*) the chapel as a site for meditation, (*d*) the presence of traditional Catholic doctrines, and (*e*) the reception of sacraments.

Predictably, relinquishing the Thursday night atmosphere creates a feeling of unpredictability that is reinforced throughout the initiation by similar procedures designed to jolt the candidates. The style and content of the rollos, which encapsulate in fifteen presentations the cursillo doctrine, are also intended to catch the candidates off-guard. Rollos are given in a room where candidates sit around tables bearing the names of particular saints. Each table, called a *decuria*, consists of ten individuals who remain grouped for every rollo. Although there are ten persons per decuria, only eight are initiates, for the other two are team members, and their identities are re-

Living Cursillo

vealed only at the moment they present their rollos. In the same room sit the rector, the spiritual director, and the assistant spiritual director, who observe the workings of the weekend, noting points of confusion and assessing the general response of initiates.

Since candidates are unprepared for the rollos, both in style and in format, many are astonished by the openness, forcefulness, and joy of the rollos. Again, this unexpectedness is programmed by the leaders to reach their goals.

> The environment of the Cursillo, at this initial moment, is marked by a complete disorientation of the cursillistas, caused by their lack of knowledge of what the Cursillo is to be and by the diverse and contrary impressions that they have probably already gained.
>
> The distribution by "Decurias" will probably have added to the disorientation; the termination of the period of silence and the first contacts with instructors and companions, generally strangers to them, will contribute also to the disorientation in the new environment that is beginning to be created.[9]

In speaking about the cursillo vision, its initial presentation occurs in the talks. It is here that the way of being Christian and the ideals are first formulated. This image entails a dual foundation: a theological and doctrinal basis and an experiential and personal dimension. The talks by the clergy present the theology of Christian living, while the lay persons illustrate how this theological life permeates their lives. These two threads run throughout the initiation with the interweaving of priests and lay persons as speakers. The clergy's presence attests to the significant

Description of the Cursillo

role of doctrine, as well as the acknowledged role of priests in this lay movement. In the cursillo, the role of priest is not eliminated nor is the central role as minister and sacramental mediator denied. Though most of the talks are delivered by the laity, there is room and reason for the clergy. It is both symbolic and instructive that priests present some rollos because it acknowledges their position as explicators of Christian doctrine.

An analysis of the rollos illustrates the thought given to each presentation. No talk is narrated without a definite reason, and each is an interlocking part of a larger system, an expression of a specific theme for one of the three days. The topic of the first day is proclamation; here the message is the reality of a vision, the potential of the individual, and the Christian dimension of life. This motif marks each of the five rollos of the first day: "Ideal," "Grace," "Laymen in the Church," "The Holy Spirit," and "Piety."

Friday begins with the rollo on "Ideal," which takes place after breakfast. The rector generally precedes the talk with a prayer addressed to the Holy Spirit, and when individuals are seated in their proper decuria, the first rollo commences. The lecture stresses the necessity of ideals in life since they render guidance, optimism, and a sense of purpose. Each person is sketched as having a spiritual dimension that, like the body, needs proper attention. This rollo is a call to be fully human, and individuals are encouraged to raise the question, What is my ideal? This address purposefully skirts religious issues by placing ideals in a humanistic perspective and discussing the consequences of a life bereft of ideals.

The second rollo situates the ideals in a religious context by emphasizing the function of grace in sanctifying people. Grace, as the reflection of God and the condition for spiritual friendship, is characterized as essential for saintliness since it is the basis for brotherhood and sisterhood with Christ. There is a continual reference to life in grace as the supreme ideal, one worth living for and dying for, if necessary.

Following lunch and a period of relaxation, the third rollo, entitled "Laymen in the Church," is introduced. Here the church is depicted as the locus of grace and the repository of Truth. Effort is made to depict the laity as necessary and active members of this religious structure with a plea for greater participation. Members detect they not only belong to the church but also constitute the church and, as such, have an individual responsibility to this body. People of God, they hear, are people of the church.

At midafternoon, the fourth talk, "The Holy Spirit," previously called "Actual Grace," points to the necessity of receiving divine aid to carry out any mission. This help is given through the Holy Spirit, but individuals are reminded they must be receptive and open to this grace. It is not bestowed on people who turn away from God, but to those who move toward him. The cursillo is acknowledged as a spiritual context marked by actual grace, available to those who respond.

The fifth talk, "Piety," concludes the first phase, and it is a key talk in the methodology of the cursillo. It begins by attacking the false notions of piety which can occur in traditional Catholicism as characterized in (*a*) "the saint," (*b*) "the fringe," and (*c*) "the pharisee." This is followed by listing the positive aspects of piety derived from knowledge, love, and sacrifice. Thus piety is joyful, spontaneous, and informal. The contrast with traditional Catholic notions of piety is striking, leading candidates to rethink their previous definitions and to see piety as an

Description of the Cursillo

important ideal.

With the piety talk, the first phase, involving the proclamation of the message, ends. All five rollos have purposely centered on the individual, encouraging each person to confront his or her past religious notions. Individuals are led to rethink who they are, who they have been, and what their religious lives have entailed. They are told of the importance of ideals, reminded of actual and habitual grace, and directed to a greater participation in the church. Through these talks, the candidates realize the need for change in the church and sense that they, themselves, are the locus for renewal. It is they who receive grace, they who can act, and they who must decide to change. Covertly, the lecturers themselves exemplify these changes and provide the evidence that transformations are possible.

In many ways, the first day attempts the same goal as the first meditation of Thursday evening, "Know Yourself," except that the style of the rollos differs significantly from the retreat meditation. The most significant contrast, which is the cursillo difference, lies in the witnessing of team members. Thus, the first day is a day of proclamation, of cursillo ideas, perspectives, and language. For the cursillo speaks out not only from the head, but also from the heart. The fusion occurs dramatically and powerfully in the talks where the team members include both dimensions.

Each rollo involves not only doctrine but is also pointedly concerned with witnessing. It is the experience of each team member; the individuals disclose what is meaningful in their lives and what the religious dimension entails. It is the person, giving voice to the spiritual and sharing their personal selves with others. It is the giving of words, spoken not only from an objective, intellectual position but also from the depths of their emotional, private selves. Each rollo, then, is a witness to the power of religion in their lives and the offering of a personal disclosure that strikes many because of its honest revelation, the gift of words that come from the self, not easily, but with difficulty and the shyness of revealing what generally is marked by a guardedness. Especially in a society where religion is considered private and spiritual feelings remain undisclosed, the rollos break this norm, and the shock of personal revelation overwhelms many candidates.

In this way, each rollo is a witness to being a Christian. The talk not only explains an idea, it implicitly exhibits it in the presentation. For without doubt, the cursillo understands the power of disclosure, of revealing one's feelings in the process of communication. Members are encouraged to give voice to their emotions and to their response to the other, and to disclose themselves in a gift-giving act. Throughout the movement, from initiation to the Workshop of Christian Leadership, one significant theme is the need to witness and to share. It is the understanding that words need not be trite nor cliche, but that words can dramatically affect another, for within speech lies the possibility of being. Within language, and within the rollos, lies the potential for religious praxis.

With the message of the first day proclaimed, the seccond day begins the theme of conversion. Grasping and experiencing the cursillo vision is the direct goal of the Saturday program. The talks of "Study," "Sacraments," "Action," "Obstacles to a Life in Christ," and "Leaders," and the fourth meditation on the Figure of Christ demonstrate and illustrate Christianity and finally, when successful, initiate a transformation in the participants. The goal is a changed Christian—the creation of a renewed self, and the surfacing of a more fully responsive person.

Awareness of the new self involves the candidates' discovery of their own spiritual and human potential. The cursillo attempts to disclose and to free this dimension within the candidate, a person who typically encountered religion through ritual and belief, yet was not deeply touched by the experience of religion. The cursillo creates an environment that, potentially, can lead to a profound experience, that is, to *being* religious. In the cursillo, Christ is not a principle to be believed, but the experience of his divine and human being. Candidates are led to the possibility of experiencing Christ and becoming themselves vital spiritual persons.

The talks of the second day carve out an atmosphere for conversion; the themes, issues, and witnessing are shaped to uncover this hidden spiritual self so that it may be freed and actualized. The rollo on "Study" makes clear that religion must be known, not only practiced. To know one's religion is to be engaged in an in-depth examination of Christianity based on one's head as well as one's heart. As a first step, one must study and examine religion to understand it.

The individual is pressed to see the dynamics of religion in social interactions and dialogues as well as in attendance at Mass. A good Christian is not only one who attends rituals but also one who is active, committed, and searching. Here candidates confront the inadequacy of religious understandings based on the catechism teachings of their childhood. The disjunction between their mature adult knowledge of the world and their frequently childlike interpretations of religion are highlighted. Religion, they are told, if it is to be dynamic and "true," cannot rest on childlike images and action.

Frequently, military analogies derived from the pilgrimage preparation in Mallorca are used: "He who can be a general is not allowed to remain a sergeant." Cowardice, ignorance, and childishness can be overcome, according to this rollo, by employing the resources at one's disposal: the Gospel, lectures, study groups, and books.

The second rollo on "Sacraments" is a lengthy presentation on encountering the person of Christ through spiritual gifts. The sacraments are defined as holy and effective outward signs signifying the presence of grace. This leads to a narration on signs, including those that arise from natural phenomena, such as smoke indicating fire, and those signs that arbitrarily indicate certain meanings. In addition, this presentation returns to the themes of the first phase, especially in the rollos on habitual and sanctifying grace. Here grace is linked to the sacraments of baptism, matrimony, and holy orders, which confer an increased dimension to grace. Individuals are left with the recommendation for a boundless love and a complete surrender as they "pledge themselves to a new life."

The rollo which occurs Saturday afternoon is termed "Action." Although it is the third talk in the second phase, it begins a transition to the third phase of the initiation. This talk explores the proper action for Christians and it suggests avenues for attaining a militant Christianity. It avoids listing specific activities but instead declares action an outgrowth of grace. Candidates hear that they must be as Christ, returning to piety and study as guides to their behavior. To be active and living testaments to their religious beliefs, they must be witnesses to the living Christ. Therefore, the cursillistas must enlarge their activity by "Christianizing" environments and searching for other Christians; they are told emphatically that where there is no action, there is no life.

Description of the Cursillo

In midafternoon, the fourth rollo, "Obstacles to the Life in Grace," is set forth. Here difficulties in maintaining an active Christian life are probed with a discussion of the laws that are basic to nature and to men and women. What is declared is that rules are a necessary part of life, not a burden. For this reason, when the ten commandments are broken, they generate a void in terms of grace and, as such, must be a central part of life. Basically it is a talk assessing the difficulties of maintaining grace, marked with encouraging words to obey the rules of the church.

The final rollo on Saturday, "Leaders," like the rollo on action, completes the transition to phase three. This lecture centers on the qualities of Christian leaders, namely, understanding, competency in assessing their environments, empathy, initiative, and generosity. These qualities must be coupled with the spiritual aspects of a living faith: humility, hope, and charity.

The second phase, then, emphasizes the individual and his or her environment, with a special focus on the Christianization process. The goal of the second day is to drive the truth of the cursillo deeply within the individual so that the person *experiences* Christianity. It is designed to encourage a receptivity to Christianity and to produce a transforming religious experience. The aim is no other than "living cursillo" which means "living Christianity."

One activity, marking the second day, in addition to the presentation of rollos, is the ritualized gift giving called palanca. This ritual purposefully catches the candidates off-guard as they receive letters, cards, posters, and a variety of objects. Palanca are symbolic offerings to candidates implying some sacrifice by the giver and handed to the candidate as a public statement of caring. These gifts

Living Cursillo

of caring are from individuals the candidates are acquainted with and those who are strangers. Palanca are offerings of Christain love, symbolically expressed in the various gifts. In some ways, palanca are similar to traditional Catholic sacrifices, but a significant difference is the carrying out of the offering for the successful initiation of the candidate, as well as the public disclosure of the sacrifice.

There are three different types of palanca, each of which entails a simple and an elaborate dimension. The first expression of caring, in the simple format, involves a note to the candidate simply communicating the message that they are being thought of. Frequently an individual uses a greeting card and inscribes some added thoughts. The candidates realize, simply yet directly, that someone outside the sphere of initiation is thinking about them and will continue to keep them in mind until Sunday evening. An example of this is the following:

Allen:

So great to have you making Cursillo this weekend. Another Apostle of Christ hits the front line of life.

We all need you and your renewed strength to try to bring about the Encounter of Christ to others. We all have Him and must help show Him.

Be yourself, and you will be loved.

Share your beautiful self.

De Colores,
Elizabeth Harkins

Description of the Cursillo

But many are more elaborate. Sometimes complex designs and colors sweep across the card; artistic sketches cover the once empty pages. Butterflies, flowers, happy faces, and a range of images weave together an expression of concern. For those with a poetic sense, the communication may be a poem composed especially for one of the candidates. Or individuals may create elaborate posters and wall banners that generally involve a group project, coming from the candidate's family and friends or from a grouping of cursillistas in the person's parish or diocese. Yet whether simple or elaborate, the main characteristic of the first type of palanca is the emphasis on the communication of care. It is an expression of caring, first and foremost.

In the second type of palanca the emphasis is on the specific sacrifice performed. Here individuals are actively carrying out or abstaining from some action for the candidate. It may be the offering of a rosary, attendance at Mass, or the renunciation of some pleasure. In the simple form, action is limited to a few, not too time-consuming, ascetic practices done for the intentions of the candidate. Consider these simple palanca:

Sarah:

May you be one with Christ on this your weekend. A very special thought for you Sarah. I made my cursillo with your husband Rodney. My palanca for you is a special prayer each morning and evening.

Richard

Living Cursillo

Dear Mr. Foucault:

An encounter with Christ during the Easter season should truly be a joyful experience. My special palanca for you will be each step I take for the next four days. I will tell Brother Christ they are a way of saying take special care of Dennis.

God be with you,
Rebecca Stilson

The following palanca from a priest also illustrates this category:

Dear Kent:

I hope that you will experience the joy that God sends to you this cursillo.

We need to turn the world to Christ, and you can help to turn it by the effort you give these few days.

As my palanca I will say Mass each day for your Cursillo. Special palance as well.

Peace,
Fr. Joe Fernandes

In the elaborate dimension of sacrifice, there is an increase in the ascetic quality of the acts, demanding greater renunciation and sacrifice. The time and attention devoted to carrying out these sacrifices are more extensive and may include a significant portion of the weekend. In this way, the sacrifices of people outside initiation are

Description of the Cursillo

symbolically related to the actions of the candidates as they are being thought about during the entire weekend. Here palanca is not limited to one day, but may extend to the entire three days.

> De colores.　　May Christ find a place in your heart forever.
> My palanca:　　3 Masses
> 　　　　　　　3 Communions
> 　　　　　　　3 days—no sweets
> 　　　　　　　3 days—no liquors
> 　　　　　　　3 days—no eating between meals
>
> 　　　　　　　　　　　　　　　Peace,
> 　　　　　　　　　　　　　　　Rene

Similarly, this applies to the next palanca.

> Give your life to Christ.
>
> 4 Masses and Holy Communions
> Confession
> No waterskiing
> 24 hours—no solids
> 1 hour—read catechism
> Won't say no to any favor
> 6 cursillo rosaries
> 1 cursillo bed
> No smoking—Sunday A.M.
> Take children to visit Blessed Sacrament
>
> 　　　　　　　　Martin and Marilyn Thomas

Another example of this type of sacrifice is the establishment of a communal vigil where members maintain a continual watch, with someone praying at each hour before the Eucharist or in front of a closed tabernacle. Individuals pray continually for the candidate while he or she is participating in the weekend. This type of palanca demands organization and the sacrifices of many individuals, directed to the success of the candidate's initiation.

The last type of palanca consists in the presentation of objects, where the gift itself symbolizes care. The simple form leads to such gifts as bookmarks, decorated pencils, pictures of saints and of Christ, miniature plaques with joyful expressions and colorful designs hanging on colored yarns designed to be worn on the neck. The cost of these is minimal, and the offering is a simple gesture of care.

But in the elaborate dimension, the expense increases dramatically, and the offering becomes reminiscent of Christmas morning. As a reflection of American society, some feel that the more money spent on the gift, the more highly symbolic it is of the love of the giver. Such things as desk sets, plants, boxes of chocolates, expensive plaques, and floral displays are presented to the candidates at a greater financial cost than any of the other types. Care is here symbolized in the gift, and the financial expenditure evident in the objects chosen.

The palanca catch the initiates by surprise with an overflow of Christian love and concern. Some, overwhelmed with the palanca, begin to cry as individuals at their table comfort them and share in the intensity of this experience. Others take the impact less emotionally, but even among these, many are dramatically affected by the sacrifices. And this is exactly the aim of the palanca.

> . . . the cursillista is brought up short and made to realize that he is going to have to respond in a way that he probably never did before.[10]

Description of the Cursillo

The team aims at shocking the candidates to alter their everyday consciousness. That which is generally taken for granted, now is confronted. General notions of Christian love are placed in a new perspective. Individuals are jolted, caught off guard, but more important, they experience a shock to their everyday sense of the world. For as Alfred Schutz grasped early in his work:

> ... a "shock" is nothing else than a radical modification in the tension of our consciousness, founded in a different *attention a la vie*.[11]

The importance of this shock for Schutz is that:

> ... we are not ready to abandon our attitude toward it (paramount reality) without having experienced a specific *shock* which compels us to break through the limits of this "finite" province of meaning and to shift the accent of reality to another one.[12]

For the cursillista, the shock or "breaking" as it is called within the movement, is the necessary rupture with a traditional perspective on the self, the church, and society, preparing the initiate for a transition into a different religious model of social reality—a realm with contrasting religious emphases and distinctive social consequences. The cursillo initiation is consciously structured to produce a break with the things that are taken for granted, and each aspect of initiation: the Thursday retreat, the rollos, and these palanca, are designed to achieve this dramatic outcome.

To understand the forcefulness of palanca, one must understand the power of language and Merleau-Ponty's insight that "language is much more like a sort of being than a means.... Language does not presuppose its table of correspondence; it unveils its secrets itself."[13] Words, potentially, are the most significant symbols through which we convey deep feelings, construct the dimensions of our world, and enter into its sense of reality. In the palanca, candidates are openly told that people love and cherish them. Not one or two people, not only their families, but many individuals in their community convey, through palanca, this sense of caring. To understand their response is to understand the possible impact and reaction when people say, "I love you," to one another. Sounds? Yes. Yet more, because these sounds are the symbols carved from the acknowledged depth of one's self, and because they usher in what Merleau-Ponty calls the "swarming of words behind words, thoughts behind thoughts."[14] The cursillo drives deep through emotional channels, purposefully discharging the strongest resources it could devise in its early days in Mallorca—language expressing love, both Christian and communal.

A young priest at Ocean Bay expresses well the impact of palanca and its essential role in initiation:

> It is very important. More so today, to the extent we cover over insecurities. It affirms the personal worth and validates men and women. It says to others: you are a good person. For the palanca involves people who do not know you, doing things for you.
>
> And in all the time I've been involved, I've never heard anyone say: it's easy to say I love you to thousands of people. But they are affected by the fact that someone who doesn't know them is doing this. It shows we are all related; we are human. The praying and the sacrifice does validate the individuals.

Description of the Cursillo

It should be mentioned that some use the palanca as an occasion to communicate feelings they couldn't express face-to-face or wouldn't have initiated without this format. It can thus draw family members and friends closer, as it did in the case of the man whose relationship with his brother grew because of what he expressed in the palanca. One can convey directly, or indirectly in the effort and sacrifice, that they are loved and that they are special. People realize, as a consequence, that they are not being taken for granted.

However, the palanca which affect people the most are those offered by someone they know. The fact that a spouse, one's children, friends, sponsors, and neighbors are sacrificing for them provides the most overwhelming impact, with reponses ranging from being impressed to being speechless, from smiles to tears of joy. Thus palanca from unknown individuals, sent in by a cursillo group or by members who selected the name from a list of candidates, hold less of an impact. Men, in particular, seem less impressed with palanca from people they do not know. Most men said the palanca from strangers were ineffective:

> I got some of this stuff on the second day. Who is it from? None were from my friends. What the hell is this? Maybe it's because I receive hundreds of little notes, and many pieces of paper everyday arrive at my desk. It's no big deal.

But, like this person whose friends were unaware of his initiation and like each man whose spouse is uninformed about palanca because of the secrecy rules, men tend to receive more palanca from strangers. When a wife is initiated, the husband sends palanca and generally involves the rest of their family and friends. Thus the woman is in a better position to be affected by palanca since she receives sacrifices from her husband, children, and friends. Women receive more palanca, and a greater percentage of the palanca are from people they know. Whereas the men, because of the rules of secrecy and the requirement of being initiated before their wives, receive fewer and less forceful palanca. These same reasons may explain why priests seem, generally, less affected by palanca since, having no family of procreation, they receive fewer palanca from intimate family members.

One consequence of the growth of the cursillo at Ocean Bay is an increase in elaborate palanca, as contrasted with the more simple expressions that marked the earlier days of the movement. Members who "made cursillo" in the late sixties and early seventies received simpler palanca, but as more individuals join and add to the number giving palanca, the amount and elaboration of palanca has increased. One outcome is the greater impact of palanca as individuals are overwhelmed with the number of wishes, sacrifices, and messages. With the larger quantity of letters and posters, the introduction of flowers, plants, desk sets, plaques of all designs and mottos, cakes, candy, and more, the arrival of palanca has become a celebration, a demonstration, a small carnival. However, the addition of certain objects as palanca is not unanimously accepted.

> Yet some of the palanca I did find contradictory, like the bottle of booze. Not that I'm against booze, but it doesn't fit. Also some things, like plaques already made, are easy to give. I think what is true palanca is something that is difficult, like making up with someone you detest or have conflict with. That is painful; and when

Description of the Cursillo

someone does that for you, there really is a commitment.

Likewise, the elaborate sacrifices received mixed responses. Some individuals would not perform what is called a palanca rosary, where one recites the entire rosary with hands extended, or a palanca bed, where someone sleeps on the floor. Like the palanca shoe, where a pebble is kept under foot while walking, this demands extreme sacrifice. There are those who consider this too European and foreign to their idea of sacrifice. Some feel more comfortable with prayer vigils, attendance at Mass, and forms of asceticism considered more American than Spanish.

It is hard to discover whether the initiates actually feel "being thought upon" as the various palanca are carried out, but surely they sense the link between what is occurring outside the circle of initiation and their present situation. For the palanca creates, through words and acts of meaning, a "we-ness," as it demonstrates the actual presence of a Christian community that is now speaking to the cursillistas. It is proof of this communal sense and it is itself part of the process of community.

Speaking with members leaves no doubt that the palanca affects many so deeply that they begin lowering their defenses as they experience the care of others and Christian love. For many, the second day becomes the day of conversion. Open, receptive, challenged, some experience in a way they never have before, and not being guarded, they do not suppress the emotions running through them like rivers rushing wet and alive. It is not so much that they have an experience, but rather that they *are* the religious experience, and the change is their changing spiritual selves.

A few candidates are aware of personal changes Friday

evening; some begin to feel different Sunday or even weeks later. But it is assumed and carefully planned that Saturday will prove to be, for most of the candidates, the day of conversion; it generally is.

As social scientists well know, ritual has the potential for self-transforming experiences. The cursillo is related to other rites of passage where there is a powerful creation of the new self. It is related to a known tradition of rituals wherein change and rebirth are experienced.

The cursillo weekend is the specific context for this transformation, the place where a new vision marks the person. Members are not slow to speak of it even though they know the difficulty of expressing the change. After the feared sense of inexpressibility is voiced, initiates speak pointedly about what has happened to them.

> I was born again. The night of the cursillo, it was somber. At night I took out the cross and held it in my hand and I looked at it; I was changed. Something happened to me that can't be explained. I was filled with love, and I knew that God loved me, but I didn't know it by reason or intellect, but it was in me. I started to cry and knew that something very unusual had happened. I knew why I was put here and that I had a purpose. I was born again. I realized that I am tied to others and have a sense of awareness.

> My old self died, and my new self is to see the lovable in each person and to see the unlovable as lovable. To see people as He sees them and not as I see the surface.

With these changes come powerful shifts in the spirituality of the cursillistas; new ideas take hold and certain old-

Description of the Cursillo

er ideas veer from figure to ground. For some, the impact entails a unifying experience, leading one priest to explain:

> It was an overpowering, beautiful experience. Peaceful, deeply moving. It touched my whole being. There was an overwhelming peacefulness.

As another phrased it:

> It became an integrative experience. It deepened my faith and made it more personal. It became a way of life. My faith became my priority.

The cursillo can change individuals radically because we, as human beings, can change dramatically. The cursillo gives back to some their ability to be in process, to get in touch with their own becoming. Here they speak their own voice giving shape to themselves as they communicate from levels deep within themselves. The inner doors open; unexpected breezes blow through, and the person experiences the breakthrough. Some never knew of these inner dimensions; several failed to open the door; and others searched for years looking for the key that would unlock the door. For some, the cursillo triggers the quest and the discovery.

Change means new ideas, rethinking older perspectives, and experiencing the vitality of feelings and emotions. What occurs is that the cursillo seems to

> Bring one closer to God, whatever God is. That you are interdependent with other human beings and that you are dependent is realized. Also to realize one's sense of vulnerabilities and frailties.

> It links you with a spiritual history. This society causes alienation and isolation, where life becomes meaningless.

Living Cursillo

The weekend links one with God, with the past, present, and future. It is a transformation from "I'm all alone" to "I'm not alone." Sensing that there is more to life than the physical body, than work, than coming home.

The changes are so dramatic for some people that we can best summarize their experience, as this one woman did, "It brought life to everything."

If the second day is the lived experience and thus the candidates' day, then Sunday is the cursillo's day. For it is the time to proclaim the cursillo's strength by illustrating to the initiates that it can maintain the Saturday experience as a permanent way of life. Sunday promises security for the religious experience, making candidates realize that faith is not left to chance. The vision that is before them can continue; security lies within the active life of the cursillo in its Christian environment and sense of community. Sunday is the day of introducing new words for new gatherings: the group reunion and the ultreya. Again, the theme of Christian environment and security reaches the candidates through four rollos—"Study and Christian Learning of the Environment," "Christian Life," "Christian Community," "Group and Ultreya," and "The Fourth Day"—as well as the fifth meditation. Through them the cursillo unveils its plan, with the hope that exposure will lead to the candidates' enthusiasm and then to their commitment.

The first rollo, appropriately called "Study and Christian Learning of the Environment," encourages individuals to examine the meaning of the term *environment*, reflecting on its temporal and spatial dimensions. Directed to investigate the battleground and to designate a battle plan, the candidates are instructed on the three fronts:

the self, the other cursillistas, and the environment. Perhaps more important, in this rollo the candidate is reassured that spiritual victory is possible.

The second rollo of Sunday morning is preceded by a talk by the rector. Here the candidate receives what is called the service sheet, which is a small piece of paper members use to structure their weekly religious practices. This sheet is compared to cloth, which must be tailored to the personal needs of the individual if it is to fit properly. Then the rollo "Christian Life" recalls the fundamental role of grace in religious life and returns to piety as a vital avenue for achieving a Christian experience. Certain practices in piety are designated as appropriate channels to grace; it is clearly asserted that they are a means and not an end in themselves. The older traditional practices, such as the rosary, Mass, visits to chapel, and the sacraments, are not repudiated, but it is understood that they now need to be accompanied by a burning spirit and an awakened understanding. The service sheet is reintroduced as a concrete plan for achieving grace and maintaining spiritual existence. Initiates are reminded that these practices are not synonymous with grace, but pathways directing them toward an active Christian life.

In the next rollo, "Christian Community," the candidates are notified that "we are part of His master plan" and have an individual responsibility to Christ and to his brothers and sisters to carry out this plan. The rollo stresses a responsibility to other Christians and a duty to attend to their social needs: "The desire to love is the most fundamental passion. We, as Christians, must spread out love with everyone we meet." Moreover, this talk restates the need for a militant Christianity, which is portrayed as a dynamic Christian spirit manifested in proselytizing and social action. There can be no doubt that the cursillo opposes any religion relegated to a stagnant bureaucratic structure, devoid of dynamism and spirit. Here the methods of achieving this positive Christianity rest on the tripod of piety, study, and action. Just as natural life relies on breathing, the spiritual life, they are told, inhales piety and study while exhaling action.

The fourth rollo, "Group and Ultreya," once called "Total Security," serves to reconfirm the continuation of enthusiasm and spiritual commitment after initiation. Realizing that many feel unsure about sustaining their newfound enthusiasm, fearing it will disappear when the weekend terminates, this rollo emphasizes the continuity between the experience of initiation and the period following it. This occurs by introducing the existence of the group reunion, which is a weekly meeting of members committed to Christian love and sharing. Initiates discover the importance of contact with Christ and with the brothers and recognize that the weekly meetings can sustain some of the fervor of initiation. At the conclusion of the rollo, instructors demonstrate the structure and process of a typical group reunion.

When this rollo is completed, a critical talk begins, "The Fourth Day." This talk is the transition between the cursillo weekend and the remainder of the candidate's life. It consists of a member's affirmation of the continuance of the cursillo spirit by demonstrating its impact in his or her life. This rollo is presented with the aim of eliciting a response from the candidates; the witness of this team member calling forth the witness of all the initiates. As such, it establishes the transition between receiving, which defines the role of a candidate, and giving to others, which marks the state of being a cursillista.

"The Fourth Day" is framed as an intimate testimony where the lecturer provides personal experiences to exemplify the message of this unusual rollo. The speaker is enthusiastic and definitive, intending to demonstrate that Christian joyfulness can be, and is, sustained after initiation. The last note of the rollo is that "life is a perennial cursillo" and that candidates can expect the atmosphere of joy, enthusiasm, trust, and brotherly and sisterly love to continue long after initiation is over.

The weekend, which has been centered on the candidates' needs, now terminates with a shift of emphasis to their responsibility, their accountability. The first such request is that they witness to the past weekend; they will be encouraged to disclose the words which affirm that the weekend has been successful as a method of conversion.

"The Fourth Day" is the last rollo, and with its completion, the essential aspects of the cursillo method and way of life have been presented. Certain points may need further elaboration, but the basic tenets of cursillo have been formulated in these fifteen rollos. But the cursillo does not conclude with "The Fourth Day." Instead, this final rollo ushers in the last aspect of initiation, the clausura, which is the final gathering of initiates. The clausura, as with the retreat phase, the palanca, and the presentation of rollos, continues the element of shock.

By the time the fourth day talk is finished, initiates, now accustomed to the cursillo style, do not expect any new surprises on this weekend. They catch sight of the approaching end of initiation, but attend to nothing more than a final goodbye. At Ocean Bay, initiates are directed to a large room. As the doors open, hundreds of people rush through to welcome the initiates into the cursillo membership. Spouses, friends, family members, neighbors, parishioners, acquaintances, and those strangers who have written palanca meet face-to-face. It is a moment of friendship, harmony, intense emotional responses and Christian love as people embrace intoning the by now familiar phrase: de colores. Initiates are held, hugged, and welcomed; here new members and older ones assemble, come in contact and partake in the circle of this spiritual community.

In the commotion of the clausura, new members begin their integration into the cursillo community; they individually communicate to all present the personal meaning of the weekend experience. Candidates convey publicly to all assembled the depth of their feelings and the spiritual breakthroughs they have experienced. For the initiates, this witnessing is an unexpected response; yet for those at the clausura who are already members, it is the reason for their arrival.

This is what the team has planned for from the day a date for the weekend was selected, when the rectora was named and chose the palanca lady and then the rest of the team. All the work, the preparation, and the formation of the team has been for this moment, the witnessing by new members that serves to illustrate conversion and the presence of renewed spiritual selves. This has been the goal that all the rollos aimed at and for which all the palanca were offered. What members have wanted is none other than the dawning of a vital spirituality, the acclamation that a deeply experienced transformation has occurred because of and through initiation.

As the clausura terminates and candidates depart, wearing crosses inscribed with the words Christ Is Counting on You, they shift from the status of initiate to that of cursillista, simultaneously advancing into the postcursillo world of the "fourth day."

Description of the Cursillo

Notes

1. J. Hervas, *Leaders' Manual for Cursillos in Christianity,* trans. C. Portnoff and M. Escudero (Phoenix: Ultreya Press, 1964), p. 85.

2. Ibid.

3. Ibid.

4. Ibid., p.86.

5. Ibid., p. 90.

6. M. Maldonado, "'I Went to a Cursillo.' Testimony of a Layman," *Christ to the World,* 6(1964), p. 489.

7. Ibid., p. 491.

8. M. Mead, "Ritual and Social Crisis," in *The Roots of Ritual,* ed. J. Shaughnessey (W. B. Eerdmans, 1973), p. 87.

9. Hervas, *Leaders' Manual,* p. 94.

10. Clark, S. and Martin, R. "An Overview of the Cursillo Talks," mimeographed, p. 2.

11. A. Schutz, *Collected Papers I: The Problem of Social Reality* (The Hague: Martinus Nijhoff, 1967), p. 231–32.

12. Ibid.

13. M. Merleau-Ponty, *Signs,* trans. R. McCleary (Evanston: Northwestern University Press, 1964), p. 43.

14. Ibid., p. 20.

CHAPTER 4

THE FOURTH DAY:

CONVERSION AND

THE NEW COMMUNITY

Description of the Cursillo

"What we call the beginning is often the end/And to make an end is to make a beginning." T. S. Eliot's words fittingly reflect the conclusion of initiation and the unfolding of the fourth day world. For the initiates, the Monday following initiation is termed the fourth day, and it introduces a period of transition back to the mundane world, a life separate from rollos, decurias, rectoras, and palanca. Generally, it is a world unchanged in any radical way since the initiates' separation from it four days earlier. It is a social world of friends, spouses, relatives, and associates who perhaps will react quizically to the candidates who behave differently than they did before initiation.

For many at Ocean Bay, the day following initiation is the most troublesome, since many candidates are exhausted, enthused, and reeling with the events of the weekend. Many discover the difficulty of making a transition from the joyful and intense atmosphere of the cursillo to the more somber and formal behavior associated with their working worlds. For this reason, individuals are encouraged to take the day off from work if possible. Those who cannot are warned to expect confusion and bewilderment.

The fourth day, however, refers not only to the Monday after initiation; it is also a term applied to every day following initiation. Each day of the candidate's life is his and her fourth day; and, in fact, the weekend exists as a preparation for the fourth day—the time of battle, the period of commitment, the day of Christian living. The term fourth day conveys a new sense of time, distinguishing precursillo from postcursillo life. The past is precursillo, marked by narrow Christian understanding, rooted in a more individualistic Christianity. It is the time of a more lifeless spirituality with unclear perspectives, as contrasted with present cursillo life where piety, action,

The Fourth Day

and study afford a new religious dimension. In this way, the fourth day is a time of hopeful and alive Christianity, distinguished by a deep personal faith.

The fourth day also functions to remind individuals of their inability to return to precursillo time. Since life is always the fourth day, there is no way of returning to the first day. Therefore, one cannot make a second cursillo, for it is a once in a lifetime experience. The cursillo is not a yearly experience to increase Christian living, but a rite of passage which marks the candidate for life. Within the movement, the fourth day signifies a new temporal dimension where the past and the present are clearly distinguished. Prior to initiation, a person's life is considered to be more self-oriented, and shaped by the traditional Catholic ideas. Now, in the fourth day, there is an unaccustomed mode of action, a renewed world, and this phase reflects the assumed change. Yet the fourth day is not only the present dimension; it is the future as well. In the movement, one never leaves the fourth day, it is today and every other day of one's life. What is left behind is the past, with its indifferences and spiritless action.

We may ask, Why the need to institute the fourth day with its focus on time? The fourth day reveals to members that the time of the cursillo and, likewise of their new community, is not the same temporal dimension as that experienced in their previous everyday world. It is not the time of clocks, calendars, nor even the sequence of traditional Catholic liturgical calendars. There is a new chronology, one formulated and given shape in the movement, understood by other members, and based on the community itself. Outside the movement, there is no fourth day, but within, it exists and demands action and thought consistent with the cursillo ideals. The fourth day is the day of pilgrimage, when all members struggle to remain in a constant state of conversion, moving toward a deeper union with Christ. Thus the postcursillo is a phase of continuing to harbor the pilgrim state, the "church on the march."

What occurs, as Izquierdo mentions in his mimeographed article, is that "the newly converted is somewhat of a stranger," and perhaps more significantly, "the world which he now enters looks upon him as a stranger."[1] The cursillista is a stranger in a world of different values, in a society more materialistic, more secular, and less intense than the cursillo world. Now more attuned to optimism, spirit, and Christ, the cursillistas speak a language that is not generally understood nor well received. Even within the perimeters of one's parish, of those labeled religious, the new cursillista can still be a curiosity, an eccentricity. Home seems strange, the parish community less communal, traditional religion less religious, Catholicism less Catholic. The basis of home shifts; allegiances are altered. The cursillista becomes a pilgrim.

How is the cursillista to handle this? Izquierdo insightfully tells us, "The newly converted must take on the mind-set of an immigrant, as one who has been deported."[2] It is the attitude of one who lives in the fourth day, in preparation for the "fifth day" which occurs after death.

From another angle, the fourth day implies the necessity of the three days of initiation. It is assumed that candidates cannot enter the fourth day without having progressed from the first to the third day. Why are the preceding days necessary for entrance into the fourth day? Couldn't knowledge of the rollos, understanding of the main themes, and a willingness to follow the cursillo ideals be adequate requirements for membership?

In the initial stage of this research, the need for personal response in the cursillo was not comprehended, which led to asking candidates to explain the meaning of the cursillo. At Ocean Bay, members repeatedly stated that such a question could not be answered; they remarked that only after being initiated could anyone receive an answer to this question. At first, it seemed these informants were hedging, refusing to explain the cursillo to a noninitiate and, thus, formulizing this response to avoid disclosure. Given the tenet of secrecy, their approach seemed understandable. But as research progressed, it became obvious that their unwillingness to define the cursillo did not primarily result from the secrecy code, but was a response to the cursillo itself. Members were not being deceptive but, surprisingly, attempting to reveal a basic aspect of the movement. By asserting that the cursillo could not be explained, they were indicating the role of experience as a critical factor in understanding the cursillo. Their rejection of this question pointed to the fallacy of reducing the cursillo to verbal statements. The cursillo is not only a framework of doctrines and rituals, it is also an experience which must be lived.

Becoming a cursillista, then, involves more than knowledge about the movement and more than the accumulation of information. Although docrtrine is important, a person who has accumulated a vast quantity of information on the cursillo will not be considered a member by this criterion. An individual who can articulate the doctrine may be considered well-versed in cursillo ideology, but his or her information will not, per se, ever establish membership. This data is information

Description of the Cursillo

about the external framework, whereas membership depends on a personal response within the context of initiation. For it is the personal experience of the cursillo which transforms doctrinal information into understanding and confers membership in the fourth day community.

In this way, participation in the weekend is a critical requirement for membership. Without this, one can never become a member of the cursillo. But, in addition, it is assumed that this participation will lead to living cursillo, experiencing a strong, emotional religious transformation. Thus the lived experience of conversion is the mark of membership and the stamp of the fourth day.

This does not mean that conversion is assumed to necessarily occur simultaneously with the three days, but initiation must precede the experience. As previously mentioned, the second day is programmed as the day of conversion, and although many will experience dramatic changes that Saturday, there are those who will only change at a later point. This was the case, for example, for one women who was struck Sunday morning while attending Mass.

> I had this feeling. One hundred pounds lifted off me. It was so exciting. I felt nothing would ever bother me again. I felt the Holy Spirit. There was no vision, but a feeling within, lasting all day long. I could have done anything—preach the gospel. I was happier than at my wedding reception.

For some, it happens not during the weekend, but following it. Others discover that conversion takes a longer time, occurring well into the realm of the fourth day.

The Fourth Day

It took a year for the cursillo to have an impact on me. Then it affected me. For some it happens right away. Perhaps they have it all together. Well, no one has it all together, but some more together.

I came to sense my worthiness and not sense my unworthiness. I had to learn to love myself first and to care for myself.

But what does occur to them? As outsiders, how can we get within their world? We do not expect to experience their experience. It is enough to understand the meaning of their religious transformations. Obviously, their ability to speak about their experience is central; they can symbolically provide access to understanding, even though they can never give us their experience. For this reason, we return to their conversations about the cursillo experience:

> You don't learn anything new in the cursillo. There isn't anything you haven't heard. It's just never been stated as it is. It's put to you differently.

> No one tells you that Christ is in you. You don't hear this in the pulpit, possibly because the priest never believed it either. But you see all men as possessing Christ, and you can't rely on just following the ten commandments in an individualistic way.

> Like my mother-in-law, she believes she is a good Catholic if she doesn't do x, y, and z. But she doesn't see that her not doing x to someone should be considered. If she goes to Mass, she views herself as a good Christian, but it's so

shallow. It doesn't have the depth of the cursillo perspective.

A slightly different orientation is provided in another woman's words:

> You take three days and re-evalute your life. You question and examine yourself. It's stock taking. You forget all other things and concentrate on yourself. I made a commitment to myself to change.

The idea of commitment to change is highlighted in this man's detailed explanation of what seized him following initiation:

> It widened my scope. It made me search further than I was searching. Before I was, you could say, the "existential man" which led to being depressed quite often. There were things which I wanted answers for. From the cursillo, I realized the need to continue searching, and I found some answers. You always get more questions, but life itself is a continual search.
>
> After the cursillo I picked up more books, anything I could get my hands on, mostly psychology, theology, and philosophy. I think Teilhard is the twentieth century Augustine!
>
> I've become more liberal, and I'm less concerned with the authority of the church. It's made me question more, plus I've read more on the Reformation and the idea of transubstantiation by German theologians. I've seen the church's reaction to the Reformation and the tightening of the rules and the codification following the loss of her people. It was like Deuter-

onomy all over again, writing down every movement and every act.

I'm less concerned about the church's authority, but I'm differentiating between the structure of the church and her people.

There is one word which captures what happens to people in the cursillo: experience. There are a variety of ways that they attempt to communicate what has occurred: it comes to be a deeply felt religious experience. Not an intellectual percept, not a new idea, or an interesting sermon, but an emotional feeling, the intensity of which affects their entire self. It is as if they are filled with a difference; old expectations lay shattered and the intensity of the experience leaves them reeling.

A phenomenon of such intensity drives through their selves and takes hold of them. It is not so much that they have experiences, but that they are the experience. Some feel a sense of joy and peacefulness; they *become* joyful and peaceful. It is not an ordinary kind of joy, but one that is unaccustomed and distinct. It is religious joy, a religious peace. Within the context of the cursillo, the experience is not ordinary, but extraordinary in its sacredness.

There is an emotional component to the transaction. This is not to say, however, that the experience is a strictly psychological one. Too often emotions are only understood from this dimension, missing the more expansive philosophical aspect, namely, that emotions involve an ontological basis. When people say, as they often do, "It touched my whole being," they are not implying the surface level of their emotions or their psyche, but an even greater dimension. This is because the depth of experience potentially involves an ontological sense, where individuals realize who they are by encountering themselves in an unparalleled fashion.

Description of the Cursillo

The transformation is a change of being, of what it is to be oneself within a spiritual realm. Intimations of being itself rest in their feelings of an overwhelming peacefulness. It is a more extensive dimension, of a greater horizon, than previously imagined, and for many, this is what bursts forth. It is as if the spiritual self, either relatively nonexistent as a force before, or shallow and spiritless, now becomes a more comprehensive and dynamic reality.

The consciousness of one's humanity comes to involve a relationship with what was previously considered to be an unexciting metaphysical reality. For the interpretation of changes in their own being is inextricably tied to shifts in their sense of Being itself. It is God within them, and Christ as a powerful manifestation that now is revealed. And the illumination of their experience occurs within the interwoven nexus of religious symbols: Christ, God, soul, and grace. The incomprehensible becomes comprehended through the reinterpretation of past symbols and the presentation of new ones. The context of the cursillo weekend provides, then, both the very symbolic structure wherein the experience can arise and the interpretative structure for explaining and understanding what is occurring.

Like a person who falls in love and whose very ontological dimension is affected, the cursillista tends to believe these feelings stem from the beloved. It is one's self as loved that is experienced, and being loved, the person frequently returns to the loved one, more in love. It is this that occurs in conversion, with the understanding that there can be only one Lover. For them, it is Christ that is the trigger, Christ whose love fills, engulfs, and enters their world. Thus the searching again for the Beloved, wanting to become loved again, marks their life.

The Fourth Day

For those who are transformed ontologically and metaphysically, the experience is that of metanoia. Within the context of the cursillo, many undergo the power of conversion as they are brought to overpowering feelings that affect the depths of their being.

Yet how can conversion occur so quickly? How can such dramatic changes become manifested in such a short amount of time? Some would certainly question the honesty of the response and the reality of the conversion. Are we dealing with illusions or something more concrete and believable? First, we need to understand that conversion, whatever it is, is not related to the question of time. It is not a phenomenon that belongs to the world of calendars and clocks, but one of another dimension that can occur at any point and within any length of time. In many ways, it does not make sense to speak of how long it takes for conversion to take effect. It is not a product of statistical measurement. The analogy of love becomes relevant in examining conversion; the often repeated phrase of love at first sight cannot be easily dismissed. For clearly, love is not the direct result of time spent with someone; it is of another dimension.

The concept of the cursillo as a rite of passage provides a better point of investigation than the issue of change from a temporal perspective. In initiation, individuals explore a different aspect of themselves, a space separate from the demands of daily existence, filled with moments for meditation and purposefully structured to catch the initiates off guard. The cursillo contrasts significantly with the work-a-day world in order to foster continual reflection and to encourage questioning. All of the techniques and methods are hurled, if you will, toward the candidates to disturb their sense of themselves and to instigate a process of transformation. The years of plan-

Description of the Cursillo

ning and perfecting by the early team in Mallorca, and all that has been learned in the years of expansion, have shaped a powerful methodology that assails the candidates from many directions. Nudged, disturbed, worried, upset, the candidates wrestle with questions planned to affect them: to shock, to startle them. The Thursday retreat format, the joyful atmosphere of the following three days, the rollos, the impact of the palanca, and the momentous events of the clausura have all been forged with the aim of renewal and the promise of conversion. The cursillo is not a superficial gathering haphazardly established, but a well-structured method with a significant history and regional, national, and international structures continually shaping its process. It is this phenomenon the candidates confront, with all its momentum and the force of its potential impact.

Plus the cursillo, it should be remembered, has its audience in mind long before individuals ever arrive for the weekend. Its target has always been mature Christians and, more specifically, Catholics. The selection of candidates has never been a search for the problem cases, but a search for those who are baptized and who have generally remained within the Church. The conversion is of those who have had and still maintain some degree of faith. It is not atheists who are converted, but believing Christians who are transformed.

There is another factor to consider in analyzing conversion—many who go are ready, either consciously or unconsciously, for a change. A considerable number are grappling with the meaninglessness of their present religious practices and an apathetic spiritual situation before they attend the weekend. One cannot disregard the fact that changes in Catholicism have left many individuals caught in post-Vatican II practices with a pre-Vatican

The Fourth Day

II mentality. Many, before the weekend, are straddling both worlds; some are tottering at best. Some also remain outsiders to the English Mass, folk singing, and a more open liturgical style; these may still seem to be a script for others. But the cursillo brings them within the circle of this tradition. Less fearful, more open, their response is unexpected for them, expected by the team leaders. Thus, the cursillo, at least in its expansion in the United States, provides a transition to post-Vatican II living and thinking. Skepticism for the new ideas is reduced through the intensity of the religious responses; many need no longer worry if the changes are good. They experience the answer and respond.

There is more. The age requirement brings in people who are between twenty-five and fifty-five years old. Yet more are between thirty-two and forty when they live cursillo. At this crucial point, a significant percentage are undergoing a period of rethinking the mode of their existence and are grappling with full adulthood and the crisis of the coming midpoint in their lives. Thus it is a period of questioning, more than is typical of the late twenties. It is simultaneously a period of religious rethinking, with many trapped in the "adolescence" of their spiritual lives. They have not come of age religiously; this they know full well. So some approach the cursillo searching for the completion of a religious passage.

> I had an adult body with an adolescent mind. I had to know my religion otherwise, for it had no real meaning in my life. I felt I had to do something. I was searching for something. It has changed my whole orientation.

Although many do not use the term passage, they imply this change in the way they speak.

Description of the Cursillo

> It provided me with an adult perspective. It made my religion mature. It allowed me to find new avenues for carrying out my search in centering my life on God.
>
> Before I was caught in the contradictions of beliefs on the one hand and actions on the other and how to resolve them. I found ways through the cursillo.

This theme of maturing religiously is a recurrent one, and it surfaces in another person's viewpoint:

> When you're a child, you can't have the depth of an adult. You have to question and evaluate. The cursillo takes you out of the child's framework.

Certain members, however, realize that the question of maturity is not only a problem for church members but also for Catholicism itself.

> The church is in her adolescence. She has left her childhood but has not yet become an adult.

Thus the perspective of initiation, which establishes a transition from the child or adolescent self to a more mature self, offers a significant edge in understanding conversion. Part of the process entails the issue of religious passages and the movement from one phase of religious life to another, more adult stage. They come of age religiously. The change is one of a person who has handled a life passage; there is a sense of completion, of pleasure in having accomplished a significant process, and of thanksgiving for the friends and the weekend that has ushered in this renewal.

For those who are older and have passed the midpoint, there are other phases in the still to be examined aspects

The Fourth Day

of religious passages; other steps, which the cursillo provides access to, unhinge older meanings from significant symbols, clearing the way for vivid images, and for the sense that religious life is a process not, as previously thought, a product.

We can then say that many approach initiation disposed for the transformation. They are ready although few could say, at that point, what they are waiting for. The leaders of the cursillo stand prepared to channel their readiness. The combination, for many, is explosive.

People converge for the weekend; the stage is set. Unbeknown to the initiates, the actors are themselves. And the cursillo catapults them from seat to stage, quickly, quietly, yet decisively. The weekend is structured with planned and powerful methods of change; all of them strike the candidate with full force. The impact, for many, is conversion. The unexpected difference is the cursillo difference, best seen as the quality of life, a way of spiritual being.

But certainly not everyone experiences this type of change. Some are unaffected by this method, regardless of its history and structure. It is important to keep in mind that some seem not to change with the cursillo. There are those who assert that "I didn't learn anything I didn't already know." Some feel slightly more emotional than usual during the weekend, but their response is relegated to some sporadic feelings and no more.

The impact of the cursillo on initiates and the extent of the long-lasting effects depends on certain factors. It is less likely that individuals who are recently out of the seminary will feel a significant difference in their notion of Catholicism. Their involvement in present-day issues and their commitment to the priesthood, marked with the enthusiasm of newly ordained members, generally overshadows the cursillo in enthusiasm and motivation. So that priests who have been ordained for several years, yet not enough to be trapped in unbending ways, will be more affected than those recently ordained. Priests who have gone stale, feeling disenchantment with the routine of the parish and the bureaucracy of the diocese, are more apt to be candidates for dramatic change. In this way, the cursillo provides a second life for some priests who sense a shallowness and indifference in their ministry, but who have not found successful ways of handling the issue.

For those who value a more individualistic and personal religious mode, the cursillo may appear too threatening in its disclosure and misdirected in its communal center. Not all Christians value intense sharing of personal feelings about their religious beliefs nor look forward to witnessing. Likewise, those who approach their religion from a more rational perspective may be taken aback by the emotional level of the cursillo, considering its methods too demonstrative and reminiscent of Protestant revival meetings. The cursillo is based on disclosive communication and shared Christianity, and if these are not personally valued, then the format of initiation will cause some persons to remain guarded, if not antagonistic.

Similarly, individuals who have been exposed to and involved with other movements, such as marriage encounters, charismatic meetings, and healing services, will be less surprised by the cursillo and less apt to change dramatically. Generally, involvement in these other movements precipitates a rethinking of Catholicism to some degree, as well as providing new modes of interacting. Thus it appears that the greatest impact occurs to those whose religious and personal lives remain, for whatever reasons, relatively static and without critical reflection. Those individuals who have been indifferent, in

The Fourth Day

feeling and spirit, to the church, yet have remained nominally Catholic, are the most responsive. The cursillo becomes the catalyst for putting things in perspective. Those who have undertaken a continual spiritual reflection and who have not fallen into an attitude that takes Catholicism for granted seem to be the least affected. Part of the power of the cursillo is to break through this attitude, catapulting the initiate into a highly reflective state of mind.

For those who do enter the fourth day, it is important to note that an overwhelming theme marking their existence is the sense of accountability. There is a focus on their sense of priorities that includes their religious behavior. "People make you accountable for your life."

For cursillistas, the spiritual life involves Christian life and their sense of being Catholic. Here, being Catholic and Christian is synonymous with being a cursillista. What occurs is the focus on growth and change in their lives reawakens their sense of meaning as a person. It links *being* with Christianity; if these were separate before, both become part of one process for many in the cursillo. Here praxis, growth, and being are integrated in the spiritual dimension and what is launched in one area is perceived as affecting the others. Being religious becomes essential to being human. To this extent, the cursillo effects a spiritual praxis in the Christianization of the self.

This insight is frequently linked with a keen sense of awareness. Cursillistas sense a method in the movement that has made them more conscious, and it is an awakened attitude to life in general—the trees, the ocean, raindrops, the beauty of a day—and to the specific social configurations of their lives—their family, friends, and relatives. It is a mindfulness primarily directed to their renewed spiritual life. As one remarked, "It is the awareness of the spirit living in you. It was a shot in the arm. It brought me out to share and express my faith."

The new-found awareness means that the ordinary is transformed into the extraordinary, the stale becomes refreshed, and the hidden now appears obvious and evident. It is as if Catholicism, in some cases, camouflaged its own spiritual dimension; years of religious training and parochial schooling hammered out a spiritless and tiring configuration. It is as if the very structure geared to lead people to a spiritual end had become other than itself; the rigid guide had become the way, and the stale precursor, the prophet. With the image of the monolith shattered, the spirit and life of faith springs forth.

This awareness of spirit and life means, for many, that the ordinary is no longer mundane. What they once encountered, they perceive differently; what they were blinded to, they now catch sight of clearly. What they apprehend, they neglected before, but now it is as if they really hear because they listen with a finely tuned ear, like someone who finally grasps a flower as an intricate and fragile essence. If before a flower was glossed over, somehow now it bursts forth in its essentialness, not as decoration, nor as a weed, but in itself, for itself. Everyday life, for some, becomes etched with small miracles. This happens for the spiritual life as well: "I lived with God as part of my life, but I didn't realize how much He was a part."

With awareness comes accountability. The sense of accountability involves a role "for others" and "from others." The weekend demands time and energy "from others." But as candidates move into the fourth day, they shift from an orientation of receiving to one of giving, as

The Fourth Day

they begin to think about their responsibility to the movement.

> I sensed responsibility. That posters and banners and all are done because they care and the commitment that is there is yours to be open.... I became more conscious of my actions and of my responsibility to be open and to act.

The sense of accountability grasped during the cursillo weekend is stressed to a great degree in the fourth day. So much so that the idea of accountability is a theme of the postcursillo phase, directing piety, study, and action. Accountability, and the concomitant idea of transformation of environments, demands action; and this activity involves others.

Perhaps one could say that precursillo and cursillo phases consist of actions from others while the postcursillo phase initiates action for others. It is not that each is entirely distinct, but together they constitute and structure the sense of community found and expressed in the cursillo.

For those who remain within the movement, one factor marking their lives is a more intense sense of community. That a strong communal sense exists in the cursillo and is an important part of the movement seems related to two factors: (1) the decreased role of the parish as a viable communal structure and (2) a concomitant decrease of community in the secular dimension. More and more we have become a nation in search of community. Presently, in our urban, industrialized areas, the social bonds are weaker, more temporary, and relatively ineffective in the lives of many individuals. For many, com-

Description of the Cursillo

munity is a symbol of past life and a significant absence in their present existence.

The cursillo weekend fosters a cooperative spirit, and when it is over, it does not signal the end of contact for these people, but truly marks the beginning of their incorporation with a Christian community. Life in the fourth day is life with others and the linking of people through friendship, caring, and shared values.

When individuals enter the fourth day, they are generally uncertain about their ability to implement the ideas and the ideals learned during initiation. The initiates may be exceedingly eager, exuberant, and enthused when they depart Sunday night, yet within a few hours or a few days, they begin to doubt its permanence. They have not yet understood the continuing support of the cursillo community in their fourth day lives. One person who is especially helpful to the initiate is his or her spiritual guide. Since this person ought to be one the new member can turn to whenever confused or unsure, members choose an individual they are comfortable with, yet one who they feel can give sound, accurate advice. This individual is considered a specialist in Christian living, one who can impart knowledge and encourage greater understanding in the cursillo ideals. In this sense, the spiritual adviser is a guide, somewhat more restricted than Castaneda's Don Juan, but definitely providing avenues for special knowledge.

The spiritual adviser is not the only person designed to aid new members in the fourth day; they also receive further reassurances from the *group reunion*. Ideally, with a minimum of three to a maximum of six members, the group reunion directs, encourages, and strengthens the belief in dynamic Christianity. Purposefully established as a small group, it is not surprising to find com-

The Fourth Day

fort and friendship arising from these meetings. As individuals share what they term their religious failures and successes, strong bonds of brotherhood and sisterhood are fostered.

The group reunion affords the cursillistas time to assess, on a weekly basis, their attempts at Christian living, time to report the problems they faced in carrying out the cursillo ideals. Likewise, it is a time to gain confidence from others that strength and grace will renew their lives. In this way, new members realize that their difficulties are not idiosyncracies, but problems all cursillistas share.

Since there are no restrictions on the place of the meeting, it may be a member's house, the back of a chapel, a restaurant, or a business office. Choice of the hour and the day are open, but, once established, it remains rather permanent, allowing members to know the date of the forthcoming meeting even when absent from the preceding gathering.

When the cursillistas arrive for the group meeting, they begin, "Come Holy Spirit, fill the hearts of your faithful and kindle in them the fire of your love." Following the invocation and the recitation of traditional Christian prayers, namely, the Our Father, Hail Mary, and Glory Be, members review the previous week's actions in terms of piety, study, and action. The technique that aids members to keep track of their behavior is the service sheet, introduced to them on the Sunday of initiation. Briefly, the service sheet is a small piece of paper with the image of the face of Christ in the center; under this is written, "I am counting on you!" It reminds members that "Where two or three meet together in my name, I shall be there with them."

The group is one of the key aspects of the cursillo com-

Description of the Cursillo

munity: people praying together and sharing their thoughts in a religious environment. The group reunion serves to encourage members to persevere in leading a Christian life, as well as to provide friendship and support for each other. The raison d'être of the group is written explicitly on the service sheet:

> If I grow cold, if I fail
> Advise me.
> Admonish me.
>
> Show the friendship which
> unites us in the Lord.
>
> We meet in the name of Christ
> and for His glory on . . .
> of each week at . . .

The service sheet links the ideals of the cursillo with everyday life, where members confront the concrete religious possibilities open to them in their specific social situations. They are able to take the cursillo ideals and implement piety, study, and action in their particular lives. The service sheet reminds members to maximize their potential and to give the greatest personal output possible.

If the service sheet aids members in maintaining an active Christian life, the group reunion establishes a spirit and an environment that facilitates an allegiance to the goals of the cursillo. The group reunion centers on problems related to the service sheet and encourages individuals to adhere to their resolutions even when failures develop. It is understood that even though initiation engenders a reconversion, there can still be periodic returns to the previous life style. The older patterns of behavior will still surface, and the group is there to aid the individual, knowing that:

The Fourth Day

> The Old Adam, especially in one who discovers Christ when he has already reached the age of maturity, does not die in a single day.³

For this reason, members ask each other set questions in order to examine their past week's performance. Some questions center on their future plans, demanding an evaluation of their relationships with their family, friends, and business associates. Members must face themselves, as they did during their initiation, examining their actions and motives and assessing their religious behavior. Yet it is a self-examination where advice and comfort is provided in the spirit of friendship. In this way, the group reunion provides encouragement, direction, and confidence that Christian living and shared brotherhood and sisterhood are a possibility.

In the area of piety, one of the most significant questions asked is, What was the moment in which you felt closest to Christ? Members respond, sharing their intimate religious moments with those present, witnessing in a limited fashion to their deeply felt religious experiences. While in the area of study, they are asked, What have you done to understand better the gift of God? It should be kept in mind that in the cursillo members are taught that study makes piety more aware; reading is reintroduced as a significant part of life in the cursillo. It is an active hermeneutic, then, called for on the part of members.

The area of study also emphasizes observing life, reflecting on behavior and on the natural and the social world. The emphasis is one of observation enlightened by spiritual awareness, where the world is not taken for granted, but studied to see what is revealed in ordinary, everyday occurrences.

The third focus of the cursillo is action. Here members

Description of the Cursillo

want to know, What apostolic success did the Lord accomplish through you? They probe this question to include the parameters of family, work, and the larger social environment. It is not only accomplishments but also difficulties and problems that must be confronted, and so members also ask, With what apostolic failure did the Lord wish to test you? again demanding the full scope of family, work, and environment. After discussing their difficulties, members look ahead, setting guidelines and resolutions for the forthcoming week.

The present format of the service sheet may soon be replaced by what is called the Christian Program for Personal Improvement, which is more extensive, entailing more questions than the former service sheet. "So that your life with Christ may be more authentic, more progressive and more efficacious" stretches across these newer pages above the reviews of piety, study, and action. Although the questions are different (Do you believe what you say? Do you act in conformity with what you say you believe? and Do you love God who loves you so much?), the new format is similar to the older one in maintaining the three-pronged focus. In this way, both formats provide a way to think about piety, study, and action in order to achieve secure ways of carrying out this program.

At the end of the meeting, the members set guidelines and resolutions that they hope will be met. An Our Father is said for each absent member, and then a prayer of thanksgiving and another Hail Mary concludes the meeting.

If the group reunion expresses intimate Christian life and caring at its best, the second gathering of members, called the ultreya, demonstrates the ability to extend Christian community to larger social groups. Ultreya, in-

The Fourth Day

itially stemming from the shouts of individuals on the early pilgrimage, reminds members that their life is a pilgrimage, and that these men and women are Christian marchers along with them. The church on the move and the idea of life as a pilgrimage is expressed in the bimonthly or monthly meetings of the ultreya. This is the gathering of the Christian community, an assembly of people committed to the cursillo ideals and valuing spiritual experiences.

Although the ultreya is marked by traditional Catholic rituals, such as reciting certain prayers, attending Mass, and receiving Holy Communion, there is a critical difference in the atmosphere of joyful Christianity, in the embracing of individuals, and the exchange of de colores, as well as in the witnessing of some members. A central part of each ultreya is the witnessing by a cursillista based on the disclosure of personal spiritual experiences, revealing to others the continued significance of Christ in one's life. It becomes a time for an individual to communicate openly to the larger community about his or her experiences, joys, and sufferings. It is a living testament to the existence of Christian life and the continuing expression of its manifestations in the lives of cursillistas. The content of witness talks are stories, events, interactions, and impressions stemming from the everyday activities of the members. Cursillistas voice the difficulties and the successes they face in their attempt to transform themselves and their families into true Christians. In witness talks, cursillistas convey the meaning of Christianity, demonstrating in their personal examples the power of Christ and the significance of brotherly and sisterly love. As such, witnessing is a way of testifying to the power of the cursillo message.

What do people discover in these ultreyas that they

Description of the Cursillo

failed to find in other traditional Catholic groups? The following comments provide a glimpse:

> I consider the ultreya as part of a family. I was shy, not out-going. But here I liked the idea of merging for various projects. The ultreya is like a family.
>
> This is where the parishes have lost. We had this in community, in our neighborhood. I don't know where it's gone, but it's gone. People don't have the time. It's gone the way of the back porch.
>
> The ultreya can be effective. People all have to feel this way to make community. We feel we have something. People will see this in us. They will see it only through our living.

Nevertheless, even though she spoke of the ultreya as a family, the bonds between people are not rooted in kinship; people can and do abandon the various groups. This explanation of why people leave adds insight:

> It is a different lifestyle. It is a giving of oneself. There are a lot of worldly things, and they have to hang on and be strong. These things grab a hold of people.
>
> They don't see the peace, nor understand that "In order to love a butterfly, you must first care for a few caterpillars."

The ultreyas are important to some because they aid in reassessing priorities and afford support for the continual endeavor to live a reformed life. People in the group reunions and ultreyas share in the difficulties of sustaining Christian existences. Because of this, as some emphasize, the quality of friendship in these groups is characteristically unusual:

The Fourth Day

> You skip formalities and niceties when you meet cursillistas. There is something different. You've lived the weekend. You are part of a brotherhood, and you are talking the same language.

> It's different meeting them. A bond is almost established immediately. Your values are thus similar, and there is a basis for the relationship. You are trying to go in the same direction. And there is a commitment to each other.

> In the ultreya, you bring together those clusters to replenish and revitalize for the next month. That cohesiveness is a tool to sustain you.

And others feel that this community instills a sense of accountability.

> It is part of the follow-up. To be accountable to a group. They have a responsibility and an obligation to challenge you. It helps to witness to Christ in people.

> It is a very close unit. But one must look for a group one is comfortable with.

For many, these gatherings effect a strengthening of the cursillo ideals as the groups furnish the needed encouragement to undertake the difficult life of the pilgrim.

> It provides an impetus in what they're doing, and it affects me. There would be a lack without them. It is always good to get new ideas and people. To lead us out of the desert we need this every once and awhile.

> You get feedback. Not getting just different kinds of people in the group, but new, fresh,

Description of the Cursillo

> new blood. We need new blood and others to have the impetus.

Plus both groups serve another function.

> The weekend is beautiful; but if you don't follow-up, it will have been a beautiful memory, but that's all.

The cursillo is concerned with experience, not an abstract memory. The cursillo wants continual living of Christianity, realizing that a continual religious experience needs a structure which encourages and maintains this desire and spirit.

Thus, the fourth day provides the cursillistas with a three-pronged method for attaining an awakened Christianity. There is a personal guide in the spiritual director, an alliance of committed friends in the group reunion, and a community of Christian brothers and sisters in the ultreya. It is with these three assurances that members embark on the fourth day with hope and optimism. The group reunions and the ultreyas become the community in action and the centers for accountability. Life in the fourth day demonstrates that religious experiences and Christian community do not end when initiation terminates. In fact, what occurs is the experience Eliot spoke of, "To make an end is to make a beginning."

The Fourth Day

Notes

1. P. Izquierdo, "The Psychology of the Newly Converted in the Cursillo," mimeographed.

2. Ibid.

3. J. Capo, *Lower Your Nets* (Phoenix: Ultreya Press, 1969), p. 124.

PART II

ANALYSIS OF

THE MOVEMENT

CHAPTER 5
APPLAUDS AND ASSAULTS: A DEEPER LOOK WITHIN

Analysis of the Movement

Having examined the history and the three major phases of the cursillo, we can now investigate how the cursillo is to be defined. Simply, it is to ask again a question of prime and continued importance, What essentially is the cursillo?

It is important to mention that when I first began researching the cursillo, I thought that I was going to resolve this question by acquiring the answers that members would offer to this very question. I thought I was trying to understand what cursillistas understood. I considered my task to be the uncovering of what they knew. But, in time, I realized how misdirected my initial aims were. Although the task of the social scientist is to comprehend social phenomenon, understanding does not rest solely on the recording of what others realize. The grasping of a scientific perspective is the aim, an awareness that may contrast with the perspectives of the very persons we study. There is a difference because the actions and intentions of those we examine are rooted in an attitude consistent with mundane existence. Their behavior generally lacks extensive self-reflection.

In the cursillo, members are engaged in attending meetings, presenting rollos, and giving testimony to their new way of life. They become members and, in doing so, are swept into their new way of life; their days burst forth with their new found comprehension. Yet this occurs without any impetus to critically investigate exactly what has happened to them. They are pushed to live the cursillo, not to analyze it. This is not surprising, for in this way, the cursillo does not differ from most of our everyday behavior, which is also generally taken for granted. Considering what Marvin Harris so aptly states:

> Everyday consciousness, therefore, cannot explain itself. It owes its very existence to a devel-

oped capacity to deny the facts that explain its existence.[1]

The cursillo also owes its existence to a certain capacity that denies the facts that could explain its existence. Members are encouraged to think cursillo, not to think *about* the cursillo. They are led to live within the world of cursillo, not to stand outside and evaluate, analyze, and observe cursillistas. To do the latter is to become a spectator, an outsider, a thinker in the midst of participants and insiders. It is also to be immersed in thought, while others are steeped in prayer; to be dedicated to learning, while others are engaged in training. What we do with what we see creates the separation between us, those who join movements and those who analyze them. In many ways, this scientific reflection is not essential to the movement, which continues and evolves without this intellectual intrusion. However, it is part of what is occurring for those who do not want to take the cursillo for granted. When we take any phenomenon for granted, we fail to grasp its fuller meaning.

Yet for all the differences, we meet on a common ground. No scientific understanding can occur without the confrontation of another's experience, without interaction and exchange of information. So the perspectives merge because they are both geared to giving testimony, to speaking out about what is seen, and to giving voice to the experience. Yet we have different audiences; they have the movement, and I have a more scientific community.

Some would maintain that the cursillo is what it is. Yet "what it is" involves the notion of what is real, and as we know, reality is, in part, a matter of social agreement. In a socially created world, "things as they are," as Wallace Stevens aptly understood, "are changed upon the blue

Analysis of the Movement

guitar"[2] of definitions. No one ever "plays things as they are," for reality is the result of a perspective derived from symbolic interpretations. Therefore we will necessarily look for perspectives on the cursillo in an attempt to comprehend it. We look not to those who hold the right definition, as opposed to those who hold the incorrect one, but rather to the process of interplay among competing definitions to arrive at "things as they are."

At Ocean Bay, many people are quite vague in their attempts to define the cursillo. Some expressed great difficulty in defining the cursillo, periodically echoing the words of Hervas:

> Definitions have always been difficult. In our case, the definition of the Cursillos offers a special difficulty since . . . it is a matter of defining not only some concepts, but a life.[3]

But there is one group at Ocean Bay which is quite definite; for them, the cursillo is a religious organization which strengthens the parish structure. For these members, the cursillo is similar to the Knights of Columbus, the Holy Name Society and other national Catholic associations. Those who hold this view emphasize the periodic meetings, the interaction of priests and laity, and the appreciation of traditional Catholic rituals. In addition, they tend to perceive the cursillo initiation as a slightly modified traditional retreat.

Yet there are other members who disagree with the definition of the cursillo as a typical Catholic club. Their position is:

> The cursillo is a lay movement. This is a rather unique feature. It predates Vatican II ideas and prophesizes the changes.

According to those in this group, the cursillo is significantly different from the regular parish groups. As one man explains:

> The cursillo makes me look at Catholicism from an adult perspective. It establishes an awareness of Christ in the world, establishes a feeling of community and instigates brotherhood.
>
> The cursillo is a movement which makes me more aware of the little things of life and gives me a greater appreciation of life.

Certain individuals are adamant in defining the cursillo as a religious movement. Whether they stress the fundamental structure of the cursillo or its consequences in their lives, this group perceives the cursillo as a movement that has a significant impact on Catholicism.

The various interpretations of the cursillo revolve around two axes: a clublike association or a religious movement. Those who consider the cursillo an association point to the following:

1. Christian brotherhood and sisterhood, as well as community spirit.

2. Active involvement in parish activities.

3. The use of sacraments and attendance at Mass.

4. The use of traditional Catholic prayers within its weekly meetings.

5. International endorsement by the Catholic hierarchy and by certain popes.

6. Existence of one founder who is a bishop within the Catholic church and another who is of the Catholic laity.

Analysis of the Movement

Considering these aspects, they feel the cursillo bears a strong similarity to the numerous traditional Catholic organizations which exist in many dioceses. Others, who envision the cursillo as a movement, point out that:

1. Membership necessarily entails an elaborate formal initiation.
2. Initiation frequently engenders a reconversion.
3. A degree of secrecy purposefully conceals the initiation and the doctrinal program from nonmembers.
4. Members oppose certain practices and orientations of traditional Catholicism.
5. Membership depends on fulfilling strict requirements.
6. There is a complex doctrinal and ritual structure.
7. Certain bishops have, at times, banned initiation and the postcursillo meetings in their dioceses.

In addition, they mention the cursillo's intent to bring about an environmental, as well as a personal, renewal through its target of social and religious change.

Is the cursillo an association or a movement? Surprisingly, the cursillo is not either a movement or an association, but it involves both structures and both orientations. The cursillo is a changing phenomenon, developing from the relationship between the individuals who appraise the cursillo as a movement and those who perceive it as an association. What the cursillo is and becomes depends on the relationship between these contrasting stands. It is, then, people acting according to their orientation and against the opposing position that generates the cursillo, for what the cursillo is depends, in part, on the definitions people have of this phenomenon. Whether these definitions rest on illusion or a verifiable actuality, they are forceful determinants of the cursillo's course of development. For, as W. I. Thomas understood many years ago, if individuals define situations as real, they are real in their consequences.[4]

The definitions which affect the cursillo, however, not only issue from cursillistas, but from nonmembers as well. The cursillo is not isolated, but part of a larger arena within traditional Catholicism. The perceptions and analyses of traditional Catholics, as well as those of cursillistas, generate and sustain the social process of this phenomenon. The four significant categories of individuals who influence the development of the cursillo are illustrated in the following schema:

	Cursillo is an *association*	Cursillo is a *movement*
Initiated members	I	II
Noninitiated individuals	III	IV

Analysis of the Movement

Individuals who view the cursillo as a religious association are categorized in the left-hand vertical column. Whether they belong to the upper or lower categories depends on their specific affiliation with the cursillo, that is, whether they are cursillistas or not. Both groups I and III see the cursillo as a religious association similar to other parish groups. Generally, nonmembers at Ocean Bay compare the cursillo to the religious organization they are most familiar with. Lacking information on the cursillo's history and purpose, many assume that it is comparable to the associations they are aware of. If they see a difference in the cursillo, it is that the members of the cursillo are more committed if not, at times, more fanatical than other joiners.

There is an inclination for those who label the cursillo as an association to focus primarily on the weekend experience and, thus, reduce the cursillo to the four-day structure. Although this is particularly applicable to those who are uninformed about the cursillo, there is also another group that appraises the cursillo from this perspective. These are cursillistas who have been initiated in a center where the weekend experience itself is the focus. In some areas, the follow-up program of the group reunions and the ultreyas are not well established. Many of these groups see the cursillo as a way to revitalize Catholicism, with the specific goal of reintegrating candidates into the traditional parish structure. They value the cursillo as a good method for conversion; with such an emphasis, the cursillo becomes perhaps less a movement and more a technique to reconnect people to their parish. The experiences of these initiated members reinforce the idea that the cursillo is a religious association.

Since the right-hand vertical column in the table comprises those individuals who define the cursillo as a movement, group II contains many of the members of the cursillo, especially those who participate in the Leaders' School. There is a definite predisposition among initiated persons to adopt this particular stand, which is related to Hervas's well articulated position. In text after text, Hervas continually returns to the issue of movements, clearly proposing that:

> The Cursillos in Christianity do not constitute any kind of association of the faithful, nor should they constitute one in the future, given their character and their ends. They will have neither flag nor badge nor dues.[5]

Hervas's continual reference to the cursillo as a movement accounts, in part, for this emphasis by members and leaders. His viewpoint is echoed by those who adamantly present and defend the cursillo as a movement, realizing that individuals not only discuss this issue among themselves, they also write about it. The extent to which the question of a movement is raised among members is best illustrated in a mimeographed article entitled "The Cursillo Movement." The following passage poignantly demonstrates the importance attached to the way the cursillo is defined.

> The Cursillo is supposed to be a movement. What is a movement? Webster puts it this way: "an agitation set on foot by one or more persons for the purpose of bringing about some desired result . . . ."
> Movements like the liturgical movement and the family rosary movement in the Church, and the peace movement and the civil rights movement in contemporary America, all share certain

Analysis of the Movement

characteristics which let them qualify as movements, using Webster's definition. All these movements make use of certain similar methods to achieve their end—recruitment processes, training courses for workers in the movement, continuing formation programs in the particular goals, ideologies and means used to attain the goals, ways of reaching the mass of people through local cells or chapters or study groups, magazines, newsletters . . . .

The Cursillo is closer to the dynamics of the peace and civil rights movements than to the liturgy and family rosary crusade movements . . . . It focuses on changing men, and through them, every situation where these men go . . . . Like the peace and civil rights movements the Cursillo seeks to build up groups of men in every community in the land who will work together to change the heart and minds of other men in these communities and win the communities for Christ.[6]

Definitions generate action. If definitions hold a self-fulling potency, it is because they affect, direct, and at times negate activity. People act in terms of their definitions, and since these definitions are not neutral, people do not just designate the cursillo as a movement or an association; they simultaneously perceive it as favorable or unfavorable, positive or negative. With this in mind, the schema of categories affecting the definition of the cursillo necessitates an additional criterion, illustrated in the next table. It is the action and interaction of individuals believing the cursillo to be salvational, formidable, prophetic, worthless, and/or militant that directs, projects, and transforms the cursillo. People act out their evalua-

Applauds and Assaults

tions and their definitions when they proselytize, recruit, witness, and write; their personal performances are an outgrowth of their particular positions vis-à-vis the cursillo.

Definitions are not neutral because they provide what Marías terms a *slant* through which parts of the social world are understood and interpreted. As Marías explains:

> Human life . . . is always organized from a specific assumption, from an expectation, and this means in a direction which gives it a "plot." . . . This is why things have a *slant* . . . . Slant is the manner of being of things when they are realities lived from a vectorial structure.[7]

The cursillo is approached and viewed with differing slants that constitute the dynamics of the movement's growth and process and can be diagramed in the following way:

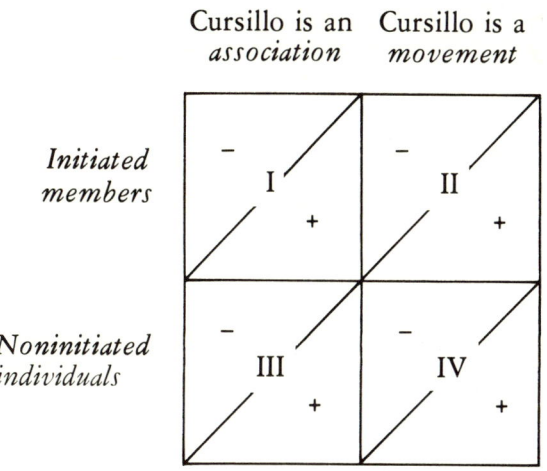

Analysis of the Movement

The various perspectives are not unrelated to individuals' differing interpretations of the cursillo history. Is the purpose of the cursillo to radically change Catholicism or to be a slight nudge in its side? What did Bonnin and Hervas really intend when they spoke of community? What type of changes was Hervas advocating? The way these questions are answered shows significant differences in how people define the cursillo. Texts, being inherently ambiguous, give rise to various interpretations, and the vested interests of each position lead to conflicting ideas and behavior.

It is time we ask, What is at stake in whether the cursillo is defined as a club or as a movement? Is it merely a superficial linguistic debate? There can be no doubt that this issue is critical to the growth and/or disappearance of the cursillo, for what is at stake is the relationship between the cursillo and traditional parish structure.

Those who appraise the cursillo as a club claim it is a structure within the parish, similar to other traditional Catholic associations. They are aware that the cursillo is somewhat different from the Legion of Mary or the Knights of Columbus, but they also realize that each club is distinctly different when compared to the others. From this perspective, the cursillo is not a threatening organization, but one demanding time and commitment directed toward the parish. The cursillo is then conceived as a means of creating a more unified and more committed parish community.

It is assumed that, like any other religious club, the person responsible for the guidance and the ultimate decision-making will be the person traditionally responsible, namely, the pastor. In this way, the cursillo directs its activities toward the parish, with control in the hands of the pastor. This model is very acceptable to clerics and those who value a strong parish community:

Applauds and Assaults

> The focus was to be the parish, the priests, and then the apostolate. Here it didn't work. It's sad, for after awhile it will lose its effect. The charismatics will take over. They are going into the parish community.
>
> The cursillo has a strong force for a weekend course and is a powerful tool. It's an important tool for personal life, but it is not viable for the parish life. I don't see cursillo becoming a way of life.

From this priest's perspective, the design of the cursillo from its early days in Mallorca is to be part of the parish:

> Bonnin's concept was to really use cursillo as a source of renewal for spiritual life and thus of the church. Strictly a cursillo-centered ultreya and life, I don't think is idealistically what Bonnin wanted. It falls short.

As is typical for those who believe the cursillo should be tied to the parish structure, this priest does not consider the cursillo a movement:

> The cursillo is an organization, whereas charismatics are a church movement. The cursillo is not, even though it's meant to be a movement.
>
> Charismatics are accepted as a church movement. It seems charismatic renewal has more divine intervention where cursillo is the effect of man's grasp for the divine. It is a man-invented instrument with divine goals.

This priest's concluding remarks summed up the central concerns:

> The real environment of life is the parish. The ultreya is transitory. It is like the difference be-

tween being in school and being out in the real life. The ultreya is make-shift.

The cursillo potentially affects the parish by weakening its bonds; parishioners may become more intertwined with the cursillo community as they join ultreyas and find enthusiasm, friendships, and spiritual guidance within the cursillo. Those who want to maintain the economic and political base of their churches and schools and who cherish these earlier communal structures, uphold the parish even at the expense of more significant Christian communities. Even if cursillistas find more Christian, spiritual groups of Catholics in their ultreyas, many priests and parishioners oppose such groups if they do not occur within the parish or if they eventually undermine parish ties.

Realizing that diocesan priests and the Catholic hierarchy have a vested interest in the diocesan structures built around parishes, and recognizing that economic and political bases rest with the parishes themselves, we can assume that when this base is threatened, or perceived as threatened, ramifications and countermeasures will ensue. In the earlier days, bishops on occasion did reassign the priests they considered too involved with the cursillo to parishes in more isolated areas. In some dioceses of the United States, membership in the cursillo was forbidden, just as Bishop Jesus Enciso banned the cursillo in Mallorca when he replaced Hervas. There is no doubt that bishops can easily influence the degree of response of their priests by more covert means. There is always talk at Ocean Bay about the bishop's feelings toward the cursillo, and his opinions can significantly direct the level of activity in his diocese.

All priests, however, do not react similarly to the opinions or requests of the bishop, since there are always those priests who are not tied to the diocesan structure and whose authority is not the bishop but one or more members of their specific religious orders. Thus priests who belong to religious orders are not as apt to be affected by a particular bishop's position. The fate of these priests does not lie within the control of the bishop, and they are freer to exercise their own ideas. It should be mentioned that since they do not generally work in parishes, they do not need to vindicate the parish structure. It is not surprising that at Ocean Bay the cursillo began with priests and brothers from a religious order who did not need the approval of the bishop to expand the cursillo throughout the diocese.

All people who join the movement are clearly not against the parish. However, for many, joining the cursillo means that they do not take their religion for granted, nor do they take brotherhood and sisterhood for granted. Many begin to be more critical of their parish and become more demanding of what they require of a good parish. Being exposed to significant rituals, they expect more from the Mass and from the other sacraments. Affected by learning and studying in the cursillo, they insist on more than pat sermons and repetitive stories from their parish priests. Thus they frequently encounter dissatisfactions with the way of life in the parish, although they previously may have held few complaints.

Most cursillistas at Ocean Bay would like to see an overlap of parish and ultreya, with the center of Christian community retained in the parish. Yet many discover this is not a possibility. This is especially true in parishes where the pastor is steeped in pre-Vatican II ideas, wanting to implement decisions by himself, without input from the laity. In this situation, there is little room for

Analysis of the Movement

cursillo involvement, for the parish is narrowly structured according to one voice. When this occurs, cursillistas will insist on other options:

> We still go to parish activities, though not bingo, for we feel the church should not be in the business to make money. But other than that, we go to the dances, to the pot-luck suppers. But we also go to other parishes. We are not bound by those fences. We belong to St. Mark's and before wouldn't have gone to St. Aquinas's, or never to the Italian church. But now we are like a bunch of gypsies on Sundays. We go where there is a young curate. He is freer, has ways of expressing himself and is not afraid. Or if he is, he doesn't show it.

The phrase "a bunch of gypsies on Sundays" speaks to those who go searching, who consider a religious community as more extensive and less contained than a parish, especially when they internalize the idea that life is a pilgrimage.

Those who still want community and parish to overlap find this difficult when a pastor insists on carrying out the work according to his outdated tenets; some remain within the parameters of such a parish, hoping change will spawn in time. Others, however, are too frustrated.

> I don't see myself as having an impact in my church. I'm not on the parish council. It's important to have a parish one calls home, but I feel that my parish is pre-Vatican II. It is sterile. I may go to different parishes to provide my spirituality. My heart isn't in the parish.
>
> Some feel they should stay in their parishes, even if sterile. I can't see what impact they have

had. Older cursillistas feel they have to be there. They wait to soft pedal their ideas. I invest more energy there (Ocean Bay). I have to look around for time and a lot of time is taken up there and with them.

Such a member directs his or her time toward the cursillo, in fellowship with other cursillistas. If their actions indirectly generate parish support or if they do not has little effect on their behavior. Here concern entails linking up with new individuals and sharing in the liturgy with them over parishioners, thereby creating a new sense of community with other cursillistas.

The consequences for parishes where members uphold this position are obvious; former members attend fewer services within the parish church and become disengaged from the general life of the parish. They may either become like those previously mentioned "gypsy Catholics," spending some time in various parishes, or they may focus most of their attention on the ongoing activities in the cursillo center at Ocean Bay.

Has the cursillo destroyed the parish? Even when many cursillistas leave the parish, it should be remembered that membership in the cursillo generally ranges from 10 to 20 percent of the parish, and their disengagement may not always be that noticeable. Also, there are other movements occurring at the same time that affect the parish, such as the increased numbers of charismatics and those active in prayer healing services. The cursillo is only part of the issue of community. Moreover, at Ocean Bay the parish as a strong communal structure has been in its last, gasping stage, with the base of community somewhat destroyed. The closing of many parochial schools, increasing liabilities, and declining membership attest, in part, to the seriousness of parish problems

Analysis of the Movement

today at Ocean Bay. Since many parishes at Ocean Bay are founded as national churches, the loss of ethnicity and the process of assimilation have left their mark.

Cursillo revives community, even if it does not revive the parish. Perhaps the automobile long ago functioned to sever the major ties of the parish community. The cursillo is not giving the final blow, but in receptive parishes it provides the sense of, if not renewing the quest for, community. When the parish is open to change and receptive to active members, the cursillo increases the life of the parish. This is especially true where the pastor and/or some of the clerics have lived cursillo. Here a pastor may discover in the cursillistas a group of energized, active, and involved members; he may sense the very dimension of religious involvement he is seeking for his parish. Just as Hervas found that the early Mallorcan lay team fit into his own ideas of renewal, the goals of American pastors and bishops can fuse with the ideals of the cursillo. Active membership in the cursillo encourages a search for community; it emphasizes the significance of brotherhood and sisterhood as part of a shared Christianity. The potential for the cursillo to awaken a parish is as great as its potential to weaken the very same bonds. What it does or doesn't do is significantly related to the leadership and condition of specific parish structures as well as the goals and ideals of particular cursillistas.

It can be seen in the table that not all who are against the cursillo are necessarily concerned with the consequences to the parish. Some consider the cursillo a threat that is even far more reaching. Such is the case for Thomas Manion and John DeTar who view the cursillo as a threat to the integrity and Chrsitian nature of Catholicism. Because these two rigid proponents of this position consider the cursillo such a great threat to the church, they wrote a book against the movement. They regard the cursillo as steeped in heresy, advocating beliefs which contradict Catholic teachings. Manion and DeTar decry the cursillo for as they state:

> As lay authors, to declare a religious movement heretical would not be within our competence or authority. But if a religious movement employs occult psychological methods, and the methods appear to provide the transition to heresy, a criticism of the methods is an obligation for any who recognize the errors.[8]

They are upset by the cursillo's emphasis on Christ as a brother and the perceived humanization of Christ which they label a denial of divinity. Manion and DeTar speculate that this approach will lead Catholics to consider themselves equals to Christ. Their opposition, however, is not limited to the cursillo's doctrine, but includes its methods. They believe the group meetings and the initiation are inappropriate outgrowths of sociometry and psychodrama. The cursillo, according to these men, does not liberate, but brainwashes. Admittedly, not all who oppose the cursillo are as negative as Manion and DeTar who are determined to show that the

> Cursillo is admittedly revolutionary. We have submitted evidence that it operates sociometrically. The parallel with brainwashing has been drawn, and the affiliations of Cursillo with the extreme leftist coalition have been shown. The similarities to secret societies have been mentioned and the revolutionary manner in which Cursillo functions is a possible counter-community, counter to the authority of the Hierarchy, has finally been mentioned.[9]

Analysis of the Movement

Thus, there are certain individuals in categories II and IV who believe the cursillo is opposed to Catholicism and who question the degree to which cursillistas uphold the authority of the church. Bishops who prohibit initiation in their dioceses and who recommend dissolving the group reunions and the ultreyas come close to delineating the cursillo as heretical. They may not officially articulate their assessment, but their actions, at the very least, indicate a question about the validity of the movement. There are many, however, who do not consider the cursillo dangerous, although they do not sanction it. They may oppose its "emotionalism" or its time-consuming demands, without attacking its doctrines.

If Manion and DeTar are important, it is because they demonstrate the range of actual reactions to the cursillo and how perceptions of threat affect responses. In the early days, especially in the sixties, when the cursillo made its entry into the United States, there was greater skepticism toward the cursillo. More bishops and pastors labelled the cursillo a possible threat; it was relatively new and part of the first wave of recent religious movements. Charismatics had certainly not influenced the typical parish in the early, or even the late, sixties. At Ocean Bay, there were occasional meetings of the so-called pentecostals, but its influence was clearly minimal. At the time the cursillo was a definite presence and a definite threat, but fifteen years later, the cursillo is generally perceived as safe, its members are considered active, not destructive, and there are other movements that compete for members and act as a buffer for the cursillo. Charismatics and those involved in prayer healing have become the newer threats.

To be sure, there is a great variety of opinions on the cursillo, and evaluations are not permanent but change in degree and direction. One cannot assume that a person's perspective vis-à-vis the cursillo at any one time is final. People alter their stance, acting and interacting differently with each new position. And as they do, they affect the cursillo's development.

The case of William J. Jacobs, a writer from Detroit, illustrates the impact of changing evaluations as he publicly documented his shifting attitudes in Catholic periodicals. Asked to attend an initiation, he takes part, but leaves dissatisfied and disgusted:

> I walked out of one of the first English Cursillos. It was held in San Angelo and I rode a bus all night to get away from it. I called it then and would call it now, a program combining all the worst features of a Fundamental revival, a Kiwanis meeting, and an Alcoholic Anonymous session.[10]

Persuaded to try again, Jacobs returned a few months later to find the cursillo at this time a more satisfying experience. Enthused about the movement, he begins introducing the cursillo into Kansas and Colorado. But in time he claims that these early English versions are inappropriate translations of the original Spanish program, and insists that these particular programs are foolish, if not dangerous. Upset by his experiences, he publicizes his views; and his cover story, "Controversy over the Cursillo," produces a mixed but significant reaction. Some readers accuse the magazine *Ave Maria* of yellow journalism, while others assail Jacobs as an arrogant defector. Letters to *Ave Maria* continue to arrive for months after his article, and Jacobs responds to this audience's reaction. He leaves the cursillo.

Then in 1965 he is asked to address the Sixth National

Analysis of the Movement

Conference of Cursillos in Christianity. He accepts. His opening remarks indicate the impact of the article on his involvement with the cursillo:

> I know as an absolutely highly documented fact, that the article served to upset and anger and perhaps even scandalize some good and sincere and, incidentally, some highly intelligent Cursillistas and for that I can say that I am very, very deeply sorry. So sorry that I have absented myself from the movement since the publication, half out of the normal instinct for preservation of my life, and half out of emotion that I might very well disturb the peace of a very vital thing. So when I suddenly got the most surprising phone call of my life, the one that invited me to come here, I decided, all right, in His own way, this is God saying, "Come back home." It's good to be here.[11]

The case of Jacobs demonstrates the impact perspectives and evaluations can generate on an individual's behavior vis-à-vis the cursillo. Within three years, this man's orientation ranges from antagonism to disinterest to exuberance. This case is not an anomaly, but exemplifies the drastic changes in attitudes that can mark individuals in the cursillo.

Fluctuating opinion bears a similar effect in Ocean Bay, where a person's positive assessment leads to proselytizing, sponsorship of initiates, and regular attendance at group reunions and the ultreyas. With a shift to a more negative opinion, there is a decrease in participation and in some instances, a withdrawal from membership. Unlike Jacobs, many who depart do not return to the cursillo, but channel their energies into new organizations or return to previous traditional associations.

At Ocean Bay, one particular pattern is leaving the cursillo to join charismatic groups. It is not so much a turning against the cursillo but a search for more heightened experience which the cursillo introduces to members. The emphasis on witnessing, spontaneous prayer, and religious experience generates, on the part of some members, a desire for more spontaneous and emotional participation than the cursillo can, or is willing, to provide. It is their initial attraction and their positive assessment of the cursillo that precipitates some members' search for more cursillo-like activities. Yet, in time, it can lead to their eventual withdrawal from the cursillo and their involvement with charismatics.

Those within the movement, then, do not hold one image nor one definition of it. They fashion different images, pieces of a mosaic reflecting various scenes. For the social scientist, the observer in the midst of the observed, how does she or he analyze the contrasting definitions? Given its structure, methodology, and focus on directing change, the cursillo does fit the definition of a movement. Yet, as Fabian notices for the jamaa, there is, in the cursillo, no easily identifiable paraphernalia, no continuous display of ritual to clearly mark its presence, no outward manifestation that catches the attention of the researcher. One must know of the cursillo's existence to investigate it as a movement. And it is this same unobtrusiveness, with its pervasive use of secrecy, which allows the cursillo to flourish without being noticed by a significant percentage of traditional Catholics. Many still do not know of the cursillo; others have only heard the name.

Clearly, the cursillo does not allow for easy interpreta-

Analysis of the Movement

tion, but rests on inherently ambiguous dimensions that allow it to seem to be correctly interpreted as an association as well as clearly appraised as a movement. Yet for all the secrecy and lack of clearly identifiable regalia and ritual, the national and international secretariats and leaders are definitive on their position that:

> It is a movement of the Church which, with its own method, makes it possible to live what is fundamental for being a Christian.[12]

In case their readers are not familiar with what a movement is, the secretariats raise the question and proceed to give a response:

> What is a movement? A movement in the sense we are using the word, is first of all people. It is men and women. . . . But it is not just any group of people. The people of Wilkes-Barre, Pa., do not constitute a movement. Nor do people in St. Jude's parish. Nor do all the 8-year olds in the United States.[13]

In many ways, this parallels a lecture given by a sociologist to differentiate between associations, social groups, and movements. This is exactly what the cursillo wants, to be set apart and to be understood sociologically and theologically as something different—as a movement. So they continue:

> Moreover, a movement is called a movement because it has a direction. It is going somewhere. It is trying to accomplish something. . . .
>
> In summary, a movement is people who have been influenced by certain ideas or ideals. It has a direction—it is moving toward making some

change in the world, toward accomplishing something. And the cursillo is a movement.[14]

The cursillo shouts its position clearly and unequivocally, this phenomenon is a movement. Yet at the same time, these texts are written for members and distributed to a closed network within the cursillo. It is as if two processes are going on simultaneously: (1) a clear presentation of the cursillo as a movement to those who are part of it and (2) the secrecy of this very fact to those outside the cursillo. Without the distinguishing paraphernalia of some movements, the cursillo passes as easily as an association as it passes as a movement. The actions and ideas of the cursillo are ambiguous enough to allow the cursillo to present two faces, two interpretations to a text, with an ambiguity it can displace when it is convenient to do so, or to leave purposefully vague at other times.

To express what the cursillo is now is not to convey what it will be in the future. Definitions since the early seventies have changed substantially. Then, much more than now, the cursillo was seen as a thorn in the side of the parish, and for some a rather destructive force. But the Catholic church, the cursillo, and new competing phenomena have altered this; the church hierarchy is more open and receptive, the cursillo less secret, and charismatics, prayer healing, and marriage encounters have entered as newer forces. The cursillo has become safer.

Yet it must be mentioned that how it will be defined will continue to be related to who the movement is affiliated with. In some areas, it will not overshadow the parish, for the cursillo will remain mostly a weekend experience, being sensed as similar to a heightened retreat. Neither will it be threatening when, even though the cursillo is strong on follow-up, the parish is designated by cursillistas as the viable structure for the transformation of environments. But where the follow-up program is stressed and where the parish is pre-Vatican II in its orientation, being against an active lay ministry, then the cursillo will constitute a greater threat. For here the cursillo will establish communal bonds outside the parish and will direct its activities to other parishes that are considered more open and viable. In this situation, the ultreya will compete with parishes as the loci of community.

In addition to these factors, one other needs inclusion. This is whether the next spiritual director at Ocean Bay will claim alegiances to a religious order or to the bishop and the diocese. In this area, since the cursillo was introduced by an order of priests and brothers not under the jurisdiction of the bishop, it has maintained a greater leverage in spreading a movement, especially at times when it was not generally approved by the particular bishop. It provided autonomy from the diocesan structure and from petty parish infighting. Within this area, this very factor sheltered the movement in its initial stages; an adamant bishop could have easily curtailed the expansion of the cursillo. Yet the very factor which provided protection in the beginning could also prove to be a stalemate in its growth. For the cursillo to be powerful and far reaching ultimately demands the approval and involvement of diocesan priests within its area. Alienations felt in the beginning remain, hostilities are not forgotten, and the desire to control the harness of the cursillo still lives strongly in this area. Probably no bishop favors a movement that is not in his control, and he will, in time, seize ways to control its development if it becomes a powerful phenomenon. If the next spiritual director is a diocesan priest, then the direction of the cursillo would shift, being ultimately tied to the bishop because he has authority over his diocesan priests.

What the cursillo is and should be is a political issue; some claim that the cursillo is a parish-based organization, and others assert that the cursillo comprises the authentic spiritual community. Many factors contribute to what the cursillo is, how it is defined, and its future direction; yet it is clear that in the area of religious movements, the cursillo's definition is linked to the arena of power at Ocean Bay.

Analysis of the Movement

Notes

1. M. Harris, *Cows, Pigs, Wars and Witches: The Riddles of Culture* (New York: Vintage Books, 1974), p. 6.

2. W. Stevens, *Poems* (New York: Vintage Books, 1959), p. 73.

3. J. Hervas, *Cursillos in Christianity—Instrument of Christian Renewal,* trans. W. Young (Phoenix: Ultreya Press, 1965), p. 56.

4. W. I. Thomas, and D. Thomas, *The Child in America: Behavior Problems and Programs* (New York: Alfred A. Knopf, 1928).

5. Hervas, Ibid., p. 420

6. "The Cursillo Movement" mimeographed

7. J. Marías, *Metaphysical Anthropology: The Empirical Structure of Human Life,* trans. F. Lopez-Morillas (University Park: The Pennsylvania State University Press, 1971), p. 95–6.

8. T. Manion and J. DeTar, *To Deceive . . . the Elect* (Reno: Athanasius Press, 1969), *p. 54.*

9. *Ibid., p. 128.*

10. W. Jacobs, "The Cursillo: What Is It and How Does It Work?" *Ave Maria* 99 (1964): p. 5.

11. W. Jacobs, "God's Plan For His People," in *Proceedings of the Sixth National Conference—Cursillos in Christianity* (Phoenix: Ultreya Press, 1965), p. 23.

12. National Secretariat of Venezuela, *The Fundamental Ideas of the Cursillo Movement* (Dallas: National Ultreya Press, 1974), p. 79.

13. S. Clark and R. Martin, *The Purpose of the Movement* (Dallas: A National Ultreya Publication, 1974), p. 81.

14. Ibid.

CHAPTER 6
CATHOLICISM AND ITS DISCONTENTS

Analysis of the Movement

It is clear that the cursillo is a complex religious phenomenon involving the ideas, actions, and interactions of many individuals, both lay and clerics. Yet to understand this movement, we must examine not only the ethnography of the cursillo but also the processess and structures it opposes. To know what the cursillo is demands knowing what forces it counteracts.

An examination of the cursillo texts reveals a continual reference to battle plans and military tactics, because Hervas specifically defines cursillistas as members of a militant army which must be properly trained. Yet these analogies only make sense when we know against what forces this army battles. For Hervas, the enemy is lifeless Christianity, which is practiced by many traditional Catholics. Hervas mentions the thoughtless and mechanical participation of Catholics at Mass, as well as their apathetic involvement in the sacraments. He is aware of the mistranslations of the Christian message and the misplaced emphasis in parish activities. Hervas observes that the parish hall mistakenly replaces the sanctuary as the central focus of Christian life, and thus he perceives that the church frequently fails to instill dynamic life into Christianity.

Stephen Clark, a nationally known member of the cursillo, reaffirms this analysis:

> A renewal has to be understood in terms of what it is fighting against. The enemy in this case is meaninglessness—the meaninglessness of Christianity to most Christians. For many of the baptized, there is no reason to remain Christian. For others, all Christianity means is a set of rules to be followed to avoid hell.
>
> Part of meaninglessness of Christianity can be considered as the lack of life in the Church.[1]

Catholicism and its Discontents

Hervas's discontent with the apathy and ritualistic behavior of many Catholics leads to a condition of doubt, with the main object of his doubt being traditional Catholicism. Since he discovered a disjunction between the ideals of early Christianity and the behavior of present-day Catholics, Hervas questioned the very methods of the church.

Hervas's doubt is important because it was a necessary condition for the formation of the cursillo. Without their doubt of certain aspects of Catholicism, Hervas, Bonnin, and the early Mallorcan team would not have spent time searching for a method of renewal. A person does not attempt a renewal unless he or she doubts the ability of an institution to attain its desired goals. As such, doubt is a crucial condition for the formation and development of the cursillo.

The significance of doubt is not limited to the cursillo, but plays a role in the formation of other religious movements. Burridge (1960), in his study of an Oceanic cargo cult, realized that the arrival of Europeans ushered in a period of doubt, leaving a feeling of uncertainty among the people of Tangu. Prior to the colonial intervention, the Kanaka were certain of the past and faced the present assured that their way of life would provide meaningful answers. With colonialism and the onslaught of European intervention, social life for the Kanaka is brought into question:

> White men have not been slow to offer them substitutes, but, with doubt in their minds, Tangu have caused to wonder which is more true, more valid, more useful.[2]

It is during this period of uncertainty that Mambu rises as a leader among Tangu. Since Mambu is able to articu-

Analysis of the Movement

late these social uncertainties, he brings these rather vague feelings to a level of consciousness. He makes the Kanaka aware of the insufficiency of tradition in providing a sense of pride and integration in Tangu. Through his skepticism and opposition, Mambu transforms this doubt into a program of renewal with new designs for social life in Tangu.

Doubt is also important in the career of Placide Tempels, leader of the jamaa. Spending many years in Africa as a Catholic missionary, Tempels fully realized the debilitating effect of white Europeans on Bantu life. He assessed the inability of Europeans to communicate with the Bantu and the misunderstandings engendered because of European blindness to African ways:

> All of us, missionaries, magistrates, administrators . . . have failed to reach their "souls," or at any rate to reach them to the profound degree that should have been attained.[3]

Tempels, like Hervas and Bonnin, also doubted the efficacy of the Catholic church in reaching its members. Tempels doubted that Catholic missionaries had really attempted to understand African life, and this finally precipitated his search for a more viable religious approach.

The doubts of Hervas and Bonnin entailed an attitude of skepticism toward Catholicism that, once accepted as valid, lead them to critically evaluate the church. It is an attitude that continually questioned the methods and orientations of the church, leaving them alert to the problems of lifeless Christianity. Because it is an attitude held by the first team of followers in Mallorca, it underpinned the development and expansion of the movement. In fact, critical doubt remains in the cursillo as a main orientation for all followers of the movement.

Catholicism and its Discontents

That Bonnin also emphasized the significance of doubt is evident in two of the nine assumptions he formulated as essential to the cursillo. These assumptions, which he termed *ideological nerves,* express the need for continuous questioning and evaluation of the church and stress the importance of critical thinking for all cursillistas. Dissatisfactions with Catholicism are not to be overlooked but confronted as a necessary step in becoming better Christians. In the words of Bonnin, what is needed is:

> A principal of sincere, honest and open-eyed dissatisfaction. This is the only possible point of departure for effective action and for serving as an inexhaustible fount of multiple and ever better achievements.[4]

Bonnin indicated the need for a principle of dissatisfaction wherein doubt is significant not only in the initial stage of the movement but also as a vital force throughout a member's participation in the cursillo. Doubt is not an optional attitude, but the "only possible point of departure" for the cursillista. It is a necessary state of mind for Christian living and an essential condition for membership.

This attitude of doubt is not directed to all phenomena, but to traditional Catholicism. It is the church that is under scrutiny and the church which must be critically evaluated. This is not to say that the efficacy of Catholicism as a whole is questioned, but certain methods and orientations. As Bonnin stated in his second ideological nerve, what is appreciated is

> a profound conviction of the insufficiency or inflexibility of certain methods for carrying through the whole apostolic work.[5]

Analysis of the Movement

This critical attitude was focused on specific methods of traditional Catholicism that Hervas and the early followers perceived as insufficient in achieving a dynamic Christianity.

The cursillo's glances toward the traditional church are not always kind. Catholicism itself is blamed for not providing a source of enthusiasm and a sense of community that once marked the earlier church. It is seen as an antiquated metaphor of what it once was:

> The Church today is like a great machine. There are many things in it that can do real work. It has all the parts: orthodox doctrine, valid sacraments, an ordained ministry. It has many programs and activities and organizations that can do great things. And yet it does not seem to be having much effect. . . . It is like a machine that is not fully functioning. It is standing idle. Somehow, there has to be a switch somewhere that can be turned on to send power through the Church and put it into action.[6]

There are problems, despair, discouragements: Who will begin to tackle them in a productive way? There is a lack of faith, apathy, and mediocrity: Who will engender a renewal in these men and women? These are the questions the cursillo raises; the answers lie in its own method, believed by members to be able to revive Christianity.

Aware that there were serious problems and alienation, the early founders searched to perfect a solution that could alter the ineffective system they faced. Yet this was before the Vatican II Council and the renewal which, some assert, has rectified the church's problems. But on this, the cursillo disagrees:

> The renewal of the Church, in many of its aspects, seems to be a quagmire for the Christian. Many of those who have set out most resolutely to renew the spirit and life of the Church seem to be entangled in the underbrush—or seem sometimes to have beaten a hasty retreat.[7]

It is felt that the renewal of the church has not always been directed at essentials, but focused instead on accidentals. Assessing its renewal, the church is seen as failing:

> Sometimes it seems like many of the efforts at renewal in the Church are like a bad remodeling job. Much of the wiring has been replaced, rooms refurbished, even a couple of walls strengthened, a new porch added, the roof patched— and now all of a sudden people have decided to take a look at the foundation and they find that they are not so sure that all the work was worth it, because it is not so certain that the house as a whole can stand.[8]

It is as if a sense of what Nietzsche wrote in *The Gay Science* is understood in the cursillo. In "The Madman," we hear, "'Whither is God,' he cried; 'I will tell you. *We have killed him*—you and I. All of us are his murderers.'"[9] Instead, the cursillo is saying, "I shall tell you. We have killed him—the Church and I. All of us are his murderers." There is a realization that in the pursuit for God, people have relinquished the search. What replaces this quest is a more passive disposition based on a greater acceptance of secular values.

The cursillo is the work of remembering what has been forgotten. It is a return to an earlier text, to an older notion of community, and to a former sense of piety and prayer as fervent and spirited. In this way, it is geared to revitalize what has been, but which has not generally been brought to the surface. Thus it is a witness to a previous message and opposed to the more secularized interpretations and values which it senses as marking traditional Catholic texts.

Minkowski has said of prayer, "Happy humanity perhaps would not pray at all."[10] Likewise we could say, "Happy Catholicism perhaps would not need the cursillo." Thus the cursillo is a response to a discontent, to a sense that something more must be happening within the church, believing as it does that lifelessness is not an essential state of being human. The cursillo began, continues, and expands because the members perceive that something is wrong and that something could be better. Clearly the something that could be better is none other than the Catholic church.

What are the specific dimensions that could be improved in Catholicism? What are the definitive points of contention? Although many doubts of Catholic practices and orientations permeate the cursillo movement, there is no definitive classification of discontents. No catalogue exists listing all the doubts cursillistas hold. For this reason, discussions of doubts demand a careful analysis of cursillo documents, namely, Hervas's and Bonnin's major texts, minor cursillo pamphlets, and mimeographed sheets from various regional centers, as well as the texts of rollos and the witnessing of members.

The following grouping includes some of the doubts which are central to the cursillo: several are explicit in their opposition to certain Catholic practices, while others only indirectly express their dissatisfaction with the church.

Catholicism and its Discontents

1. They [the true faithful] are not found especially in the parish theatre, nor at the bingos nor in the processions; not even to be exact, at Sunday Mass.[11]

2. It is not enough to direct our actions to the personal reform of the individual.... What is needed then is not a partial individualistic solution.[12]

3. ... the historical Christ Himself is not sufficient for, although He was God and Man at the same time, He walked our earth two thousand years ago. To over-emphasize the historical Christ ... is to mutilate Christ. It is to disfigure Christ.[13]

4. A pessimistic concept of the world is incompatible with a truly Christian outlook on life.[14]

5. Christianity is not a catalogue of prohibitions.[15]

6. ... the Catholic faith is not a mere sum of truths artificially connected, forming an inert whole.[16]

7. The fundamental Christianity, the Christian life of which we speak frequently, we do not understand in an abstract, impersonal way.[17]

8. The structure of Christian living is not recognized as some ritual handed down by a hierarchy.[18]

9. The apostolate ... does not consist merely in announcing the good news.[19]

Analysis of the Movement

10. The transmission of the truth from one group of men to another or from one man to another . . . cannot be achieved as though you were pouring a liquid from one container into another.[20]

11. No Christian should look upon the life of Grace as just another thing in human life.[21]

12. The exposition of theological truths . . . is not to be found exclusively in knowing.[22]

13. When we overemphasize slogans and verbal rituals . . . we often end up with victims, i.e., those who conquer and those who are conquered among the brethren.[23]

14. God, Christ, is not a static concept.[24]

These statements indicate a continual reference to the inadequacy and the misdirection of certain religious methods and orientations of traditional Catholicism. These statements, and their implied position, are the result of a critical attitude, of doubt and skepticism.

Hervas's and Bonnin's attitude, however, is not one which only questions and criticizes. It is a state of thinking which impels them to look for a solution. It is an attitude reflected in Tom Clark's words that, "just getting rid of what is in the way, however, can only be a first step."[25] What occurs is not just an opposition to the church or just the eradication of the problem, but the formulation of a new position. The opposition to the ineffective activity and the outdated procedures lead Hervas and Bonnin to draft remedies for the problematic areas. Out of these new positions stemmed the doctrines of the cursillo.

Doubt, then, does not only generate confrontation; it also impels individuals to hammer out solutions. The dis-

Catholicism and its Discontents

contents act as catalysts in the fashioning of a distinct religious direction. Put more concisely, doubt leads to belief. It is through awareness of specific doubts that the doctrinal system originates. Doubts illustrate certain weaknesses, fereting out the problematic areas in the church and thereby shaping the direction of the movement.

To clearly grasp the relationship between doubt and belief, it is necessary to present a more extensive context than provided in the previous grouping of doubts. The proceeding material illustrates the shift from a position of doubt to the cursillo perspective:*

1. They [the true faithful] are not found especially in the parish theatre, not at the bingos nor in the processions; not even to be exact, at Sunday Mass. *The true faithful, the vital ones, are seen at the foot of the altar when the priest distributes the living Bread from Heaven.***

2. It is not enough to direct our actions to the personal reform of the individual. . . . What is needed then is not a partial individualistic solution, but *an environmental transformation that will reach everyone and everything.*

3. *The Cursillos in Christianity concentrate on the mystical Christ and all the richness of*

---

*Sources for this consecutive listing have been previously credited.

**All italics are mine, and they are used to distinguish the belief from the doubt.

Analysis of the Movement

the truths which it implies. First of all, the historical Christ Himself is not sufficient for, although He was God and Man at the same time, He walked our earth two thousand years ago. To over-emphasize the historical Christ and to forget the mystical Christ is to mutilate Christ. It is to disfigure Christ.

4. ... *The Cursillos in Christianity are infused with the happiness and enthusiasm which all authentic Christian life must possess.* A pessimistic concept of the world is incompatible with a truly Christian outlook on life.

5. *Christianity is* not a catalogue of prohibitions, but *principally a great affirmation; that of loving God above all things.*

6. ... *the Catholic faith is* not a mere sum of truths artificially connected, forming an inert whole but *an organic construction by the Holy Spirit, an organism formed according to the law of a living being.*

7. The fundamental Christianity, the Christian life of which we speak frequently, we do not understand in an abstract, impersonal way, but *made flesh in individuals who have to develop their personal vocation in the Church and in the world.*

8. *The structure of Christian living is* not recognized as some ritual handed down by a hierarchy, but rather, *a "living" of present life by people who desire to act in their*

world as they believe Jesus would conduct himself.

9. *The apostolate* . . . does not *consist* merely in announcing the good news, but also *in leading men to the sources of salvation.*

10. The transmission of the truth from one group of men to another or from one man to another . . . cannot be achieved as though you were pouring a liquid from one container into another. *It is understanding which requires extreme care and discernment on the levels of spirit.*

11. . . . the constant and most urgent issue is that Christians live in Grace, and that *a life in Grace is the ideal, the great ideal held up to all within the Church.* No Christian should look upon the life of Grace as just another thing in human life.

12. *The exposition of theological truths* . . . is not to be *found* exclusively in knowing, but also *in living.*

13. *The total focus must be centered on the person. Only within this frame of reference can we properly evaluate all ideology and methodology* . . . When we over-emphasize slogans and verbal rituals, instead of *fostering true brotherhood,* we often end up with victims, i.e., those who conquer and those who are conquered among the brethren.

14. *And when we speak of faithfulness to the Gospel, we mean that everyone must have*

Analysis of the Movement

a concept of Christ that is faithful and dynamic. God, Christ, is not a static concept.

These statements illustrate that in the cursillo understanding its belief system necessarily entails an examination of its doubts and dissatisfactions. Yet if the particular doubts are not obvious to nonmembers, it is because the cursillo masks its doubts. The cursillo, like other religious systems, presents itself as a body of beliefs, camouflaging its opposition to traditional Catholicism, an opposition not lightly regarded by members of the church. In fact, many cursillistas are not fully aware of the significance of doubt in the cursillo. Members are aware of the opposition to certain doctrines and rituals, yet what is generally hidden is the extent to which the cursillo doubts the traditional methods and orientations of the church.

The issue of discontents and dissatisfactions certainly marks the social scientific research on religious movements. However, too frequently the available research examines the psychological dimensions of these discontents, focusing on the personal problems of those who join. There is a need to examine discontents within the larger social structure, against which movements move and are shaped into active social phenomena. Within this type of orientation, the story of discontents shifts from the problems of individuals to the problems of institutions, from psychological aberrations to social structures that have become static and bureaucratized, and from personal issues to the issue of language and a symbolic system that has become relatively meaningless and taken for granted.

The discontents point to a crisis, but it is not solely a psychological crisis. It is a crisis in the hermeneutics of the church; textual interpretations speak to the past, to a people with different needs; the images are not vibrant and its language is too often one of platitudes. For this reason, the targets are the metaphors and analogies that shape the religious reality through which members live and construct the image of their church.

In the cursillo, words must have an impact on individual members, and to accomplish this, the antiquated vocabulary of the church is altered. The old, rigid slogans and phrases are abandoned in favor of a language which jolts men and women to a condition of awareness. The traditional language of the church is broken down as it is renewed and transformed within the cursillo context. The question being posed is, What is the vibrant language of Christianity? From Barthes's perspective, the answer involves "unexpress[ing] the expressible,"[26] and the target is none other than the present language of traditional Catholicism.

Language in the cursillo is geared to the everyday speech of people. It is no longer steeped in antiquated analogies removed from everyday experiences, but it is rooted in the actions and thoughts that are part of today's world. Grace is no longer the water necessary for the plant (a frequent analogy for a Catholic) to grow, but grace is understood as a "now presence," a "now sharing," and a "now gift." Men and women freed from the analogies of plants and vessels, leave their passive roles since each person "must be awakened to his (her) reality." Each person is not a vessel which receives love, but an active agent who creates love. Love is dynamic and "the desire to love is the most fundamental passion." For the cursillistas, this means that "we as Christians must spread our love with everyone we meet."

No longer is one content to speak of the infusion of the Holy Spirit; instead the cursillistas speak of themselves as "Spirit People." They do not just passively receive the "third person of the Blessed Trinity," but become different, those who are part of the Spirit People. In addition, sin is not a "spot on one's soul," but a "contradiction of what love is all about." In the cursillo, sin is no longer doing wrong, as much as it is not doing enough good, for sin is understood as "a reality that cramps our style."

Language is thus important in the cursillo. It is viewed as an instrument of renewal, a means of attaining Christian goals and a vehicle of communication with fellow Christians. The cursillo's attraction to language, however, is counteracted with a caution, a skepticism for this very vehicle; although it is a way of bringing understanding, language alone cannot change Christianity. Since "the apostolate does not consist merely in announcing the good news," language in the cursillo must be harnessed to action. Christianity is not only the accumulation of new words and phrases but also the performance of action as well. Individuals must project themselves into the world; they must act upon it and be transformed by this very act. The cursillistas become Christians by their conduct as well as through their speech.

Religion is living as well as speaking. Christianity is defined as life and love, not a catalogue of prohibitions. Words may give direction and serve as guides, but in the cursillo, speech needs action, since religion is conceived as a "living of present life by people who desire to act in their world." Men and women are not passive receivers, but creative agents, and thus the stress on active, militant Christianity. Individuals must be involved in their world as well as in their religion, for both are necessarily united in the cursillo.

Individuals are encouraged to communicate and to maintain a dialogue; this is evident in the importance attributed to proselytizing. The work of preaching is not relegated to the domain of priests, but each man and woman must be a teacher bearing witness to Christ. Each member attempts to become an active apostle of religion as he or she struggles to bring family, friends and business associates toward this involvement in Christianity.

This is not to say that all action is recognized as important. The action sought in the cursillo is not the organization of bingos, cake sales, nor bean suppers, but action derived from personal experiences and personal understanding of Christian living. Members' behavior must flow from their personal reactions to their social environments, demanding involvement of cursillistas in their home, office, and community.

The cursillo also opposes rigid and formalized actions that are geared to a bureaucratized institution instead of being designed for individual needs. It is an opposition to a mass-produced religion, tailor-made for no one in particular. For the cursillo, religion must become a spiritual force and a living experience. It is the affirmation of religion as a part of life, a part of living, wherein doctrine and experience unite.

> It [fundamental Christianity] cannot be understood as something independent of the personal meaning that it takes when it becomes life conscious and growing life—in each one of us.[27]

Since the cursillo is against highly formalized and bureaucratic action, it is not surprising to find the cursillo searching for the essential aspects of Christianity. Since the cursillo's search for essences leads to its emphasis on the doctrines of the past, there is a definite desire to live Christianity as it was preached and practiced during the first century A.D. In this sense, the cursillo affirms a return to primitive Christianity, to a time when this religion was not encumbered by the elaborations and additions of the present Catholic rituals and doctrinal systems. Today's Catholicism is perceived as being weighed down by excessive elaborations, and because of this, it is analogous to a baroque cathedral. In contrast, the cursillo is considered to be

> like modern art which tries to express the essence of a thing with directness, simplicity and taste. Or it is like the architecture of modern churches. Anyone who enters most modern churches first notices the altar and, in its center, the tabernacle, above which hangs the crucified Christ suspended between heaven and earth as mediator between God and man.[28]

In this way, the cursillo relegates the nonessential aspects of Christianity to the background, while bringing into focus the essential Christian doctrines.

The cursillo's return to primitive Christianity and its search for essences are also responses to the problem of reification in Catholicism. The cursillo opposes the "concretizing" of Catholicism, where visible signs are equated with abstract, mystical power; where crosses, medals, and statues are believed to possess spiritual power in themselves, instead of understood to be visible indicators of religious power. The cursillo attacks reification since it views religion as abstract, and not a catalogue of tangible objects. This is made clear when cursillistas affirm that "Piety is not a living thing; it is living," or when Bonnin asserts that:

> We are accustomed to speak of the state of grace. It would be more proper to speak of the *process* of grace.[29]

It is this position against misplaced concreteness that determines its attack against a metaphysical Being, defined in restricted historical terms. It is a critical attack against the historical delineation of Christ, as an insufficient and incorrect approach. For the cursillo, the essential aspect of Christ is his mystical nature and not a portrayal of Christ limited to thirty-three years of history. Thus the cursillo emphasizes that "Christ is not a static concept" and "everyone must have a concept of Christ that is faithful and dynamic." The cursillo returns to early Christianity for the essential doctrines of Christian faith, but it does not remain in the past. In the cursillo, the doctrines, including the concept of Christ, must be translated into the language of twentieth century men and women, in order that religion may be a living and dynamic force. It is in this sense that the cursillo's search for essential Christianity is an outgrowth of its doubts of the baroque language and the reification of traditional Catholicism, illustrating once again the significance of doubt in the formulation of the cursillo belief system.

The general sense of discontents experienced in the cursillo, however, does not mean that cursillistas, even with their doubts, do not see themselves as Catholics. In fact, they see the cursillo as necessary to become good Catholics. There is a marked similarity between the cursillistas who visualize themselves as faithful Catholics and the Haitians engaged in voodoo who state, "To serve the loa you have to be a Catholic."[30] Believers in voodoo see no contradiction in sacrificing to and being possessed by the loa, while continuing to receive sacraments. For them, involvement in voodoo coexists with Catholicism, demanding of the believer a strict adherence to Catholic rituals. Without Catholicism, voodoo is not legitimate, but reduced to a pagan practice, and so for these Haitians, both are intricately related and complementary. If Catholicism provides the legitimating basis for voodoo, voodoo in turn, makes Catholicism a meaningful and understandable religion. Voodoo, for the Haitians, makes them better and more believing Catholics.

It is in this sense that cursillistas perceive their movement as an *improvement* on Catholicism. Aware of the lifeless practices and the misplaced emphasis within the church, they consider the cursillo a better translation of the Catholic message. As a more correct expression of Catholic doctrine, members consider the cursillo an avenue for being more religious and more Christian. For them, the cursillo is not separate from the church but a long-awaited salutary movement, capable of renewing Catholicism.

The cursillo, by defining its problems with Catholicism, sees itself, to use Geertz' phrase, as a *model for* Catholicism, a way to carry out Catholic beliefs and rituals. The cursillo is a model for Catholic community; it demonstrates a community in action, expressing care and concern. Yet on close observation, the cursillo is not only a model for community; it becomes, in addition, a *model of* the Catholic community; it presents the ideal of what religious social bonding should be. It gives the experience of community while it provides a plan, an ideal, and an image of community itself. In this way, the cursillo is not just an aid to being a good Catholic; it is the way to be Catholic.

Concretely this means that activity in the cursillo is frequently focused back on itself, that the concern with community involves specific attention to the cursillo community. We can understand this more clearly when we consider the specific area of initiation. It is not accidental that all significant role players are present at initiatión, for the cursillo channels its devotion and commitment back into the movement. The cursillo excites individuals to a militant Christianity, and it encourages members to direct this enthusiasm and zeal within the very structure of the movement. When individuals are trained, it is to be knowledgeable in the presentation of their rollos. When individuals are ready to proselytize the message of militant Christianity, it is partly in the form of sponsorship. And when individuals decide to witness, it is generally at ultreyas and at the clausuras.

The enthusiasm, dedication, and training of the members is mobilized and funneled within the movement. The cursillo launches an active, involved following and absorbs the very fruits of its followers. Initiation is one of the principal areas in which the movement uses the fervency and training of its members. It is the context in which members can put into practice the teachings of the cursillo, and it is the arena that requires the results of piety, study, and action. Members are encouraged to avail themselves of all three in achieving a militant Christianity, yet what occurs is that this three-pronged process is directed to the recruiting of candidates, the organization of initiation and the execution of its structure. As such, it is piety, study, and action for, through, and within the cursillo initiation and the cursillo movement.

Consider, for example, the relationship between the ideals of piety, study, and action and the concrete responses which typify the behavior of members at Ocean Bay. In figure 2, on the left are listed the general social and religious activity which corresponds with each major theme, while on the right are many of the specific translations of each technique by cursillistas.

This is not to say that all projects and plans of action are directed back to the cursillo. Individuals do read books

	General Directives	Specific Cursillo Context
Piety	Personal Renunciations	Palanca
	Spontaneous Prayer	Witnessing
	Ritualized Prayer	Opening, Closing of Group Reunion, Ultreya, Leaders' School
	Rosary, Visits to Chapel	Service Sheet
	Reception of Sacraments	Ultreya
	Christian Brotherhood and Sisterhood	Group Reunion, Ultreya, Leaders' School
Study	History of the Church	Cursillo History
	Scriptures	Course in Leaders' School
	Christian Dogma	Cursillo Beliefs: Course in Leaders' School, Rollos
	Self-Reflection	Meditation; Service Sheet
	Intellectual Pursuits	Read Cursillo Documents by Hervas, Bonnin, Duran, Capo; Read Cursillo Periodicals
	Examine and Analyze the Social Environment	Examine and Expand the Cursillo
Action	Leadership	Role of Rector, Spiritual Director, Instructor
	Communal Involvement	Group Reunion, Ultreya, Leaders' School
	Share Personal Experiences	Presentation of Rollo, Fourth Day Talk, Witnessing
	Proselytizing	Sponsorship of Candidates
	Sacrificial Action	Attending Clausuras, Being a Team Member, Palanca

that are not written by cursillistas, and explore philosophy and the social sciences. Some members engage in community activities, helping the disabled, the hard-pressed, and the delinquent. Yet what is important is that members are inclined and encouraged to direct their interest and their time within cursillo activities. Such a significant percentage of a member's activity is redirected back to the cursillo, that cursillo activities become a very driving and consuming phenomenon.

Given that the cursillo does channel its intensity and its élan back to itself, it is not surprising to find that initiation, for example, is part of the raison d'être of the Leaders' School, impelling individuals to study theology, church history, and doctrine in order to be well prepared as a team leader. Initiation also motivates members to undertake extensive research on areas of piety, charity, and hope, as leaders perfect their specific rollos. Thus, the cursillo both encourages Christian living and provides the very source and center in which it is exhibited and expressed.

To conclude, what we encounter is that through its definitive discontents with Catholicism, the cursillo comes into being as a model for being Catholic, with its own particular emphasis on community, action, and piety. As it forges a model for acting out Catholicism, its very structure becomes a way of being Catholic. In this manner, the cursillo represents something more, the very model of Catholicism. It thus means that instead of not seeing themselves as Catholic because of their doubts and discontents, cursillistas envisage themselves as more Catholic, as the very essence of what it means to be Catholic. What occurs is that the doubts are transformed into a system of beliefs, providing the power to generate dynamic images and a renewed way of religious life, a life intimately tied to the very structure it alters and rectifies. In this way, we understand that for the cursillistas, like the Haitians, embracing their movement is their way of being Catholic.

Notes

1. S. Clark, *The Work of the Cursillos and the Work of Renewal* (Phoenix: Ultreya Press, 1967), p.2.

2. K. Burridge, *Mambu: A Study of Melanesian Cargo Movements and their Social and Ideological Background* (New York: Harper and Row, 1970), p.253.

3. P. Tempels, *Bantu Philosophy* (Paris: Présence Africaine, 1959), p. 28.

4. E. Bonnin, *The How and the Why* (Phoenix: Ultreya Press, 1966), p. 25.

5. Ibid.

6. S. Clark and R. Martin, *The Purpose of the Movement* (Dallas: A National Ultreya Publication, 1974), p. 52.

7. Ibid., p. 54.

8. Ibid., p. 56.

9. F. Nietzsche, "The Madman," *The Gay Science* trans. W. Kaufman (New York: Vintage Books, 1974), p. 181.

10. E. Minkowski, *Lived Time: Phenomenology and Psychopathological Studies,* trans. N. Metzel (Evanston: Northwestern University Press, 1970), p. 110.

11. Bonnin, *The How,* p. 35.

12. Ibid., p. 33.

13. A. Duran, *The Essence and Purpose* (Phoenix: Ultreya Press, 1966) p. 10.

14. Ibid., p. 16.

Analysis of the Movement

15. J. Hervas, *Cursillos in Christianity—Instrument of Christian Renewal,* trans. W. Young (Phoenix: Ultreya Press, 1965), p. 78.

16. Ibid., p. 59.

17. E. Bonnin, "The Third Session of Leaders National Sharing Workshop," mimeographed, 1968, p. 2.

18. T. Moran, "Involvement of a Weekend," mimeographed, 1970, p. 7.

19. Hervas, *Instrument of Renewal,* p. 59.

20. Bonnin, *The How,* p. 55.

21. A. Duran, *The Cursillos in Christianity Movement* (Phoenix: Ultreya Press, 1966), p. 11.

22. Hervas, *Instrument of Renewal,* p. 59.

23. Bonnin, "The Essential, the Important, and the Accidental in the Cursillo Movement," mimeographed, 1968, p. 3.

24. Ibid.

25. S. Clark, *The Work of the Cursillos and the Work of Renewal* (Phoenix: Ultreya Press, 1967), p. 4.

26. R. Barthes, *Critical Essays,* (Evanston: Northwestern University Press, 1972), p. xvii.

27. Bonnin, "Third Session," p. 2.

28. A. Duran, *The Cursillos in Christianity Movement* (Phoenix: Ultreya Press, 1966), p. 9.

29. Bonnin, "The Essential," p. 29.

30. A. Metraux, *Voodoo in Haiti,* trans H. Charteris (New York: Schocken Books, 1972), p. 323.

CHAPTER 7

CHARISMA AND TRADITION: THE CREATIVE WORK OF RENEWAL

Analysis of the Movement

Without a doubt, movements entail *work,* and the cursillo is the consequence of years of effort by Hervas and Bonnin, as well as those engaged in the expansion of the movement. For the cursillo emerges as the intense work of renewal, from the time its direction was launched in Mallorca by the early team.

Since individuals do not automatically embrace a program of renewal, there must be a basis for their support, and it is this ground that constitutes part of the present work of the movement. This issue encompasses the methods by which Catholics accept the cursillo's program, namely, the process of legitimation.

Clearly, the work of legitimation is complex and elaborate. Individuals must initially experience a degree of dissatisfaction with Catholicism and grasp the inadequacy of certain traditional Catholic methods and perspectives. The picture of the church as outdated and routine-bound must mesh with individuals' personal experiences. If individuals judge Catholicism as a dynamic and life-enhancing institution, then they will dismiss the cursillo's assessment as inaccurate or irrelevant. The cursillo's analysis of religious problems must be compatible with the potential members' appraisal. Even if people do concur with the cursillo's assessment, this does not in itself guarantee a following. They must be convinced that the particular method of renewal is viable. Followers must be persuaded that this program will renew Catholicism and that it can foster Christian living through its particular methodology. The question of legitimation necessitates success in two spheres: first, in the assessment of traditional Catholicism and second, in the formation of an acceptable program of action.

To understand the issue of legitimation, it is necessary to reexamine the role of Juan Hervas and Edouardo Bon-

Charisma and Tradition

nin. Part of the reason the cursillo program is accepted by almost two million members rests in their capacities as founders and leaders, that is, in their charismatic abilities. To say that Hervas and Bonnin possess charisma, however, is not to say that they have special supernatural powers. We can better comprehend charisma by understanding it as work, as part of the process of legitimation that accounts for the success Bonnin and Hervas had in their efforts at renewal.

Thinking of charisma as work is substantially different from the idea of charisma as a gift; the concept of work comprises the transactions of an individual with others, arising from the process of creating meaning. It takes leave of a psychological focus and embarks on a more sociological and interpersonal analysis. Charisma as work focuses on the active, demanding role of the leaders, instead of concentrating on the followers as passive receptacles for spiritual powers. No, charisma is not an erratic force, or a superhuman power, but a very human capacity to reach others forcibly and to allow the images and conceptualizations of another to guide one's actions and affect one's feelings. It is the attraction of one individual to another, based on the human ability to go beyond the sphere of idiosyncratic experiences, as well as the ability to fashion dreams that catch hold in another's world. Charisma then, is necessarily related to the intersubjective work of interacting with an audience.

We can say that the emergence of a charismatic leader depends on the existence of an audience, since charisma arises through a dynamic interaction between the leader and followers. Charismatic leaders are involved with and affected by an audience when they speak out to known social groups. The charismatic leader addresses a certain audience composed of individuals with various kinship,

Analysis of the Movement

residence, and national allegiances. The successful leaders not only catch sight of the values, norms, and ethos of their audience, but more signficantly, their message reflects these very aspects. They generally draft alterations in the norms or goals of their audience, but the proposed changes entail a dialectic relationship between the previous symbolic structures and the presently projected alterations. It is not so much the leaders' negation of the past, as their use of the past as a catalyst that allows the desired changes to be attained.

Charismatic leaders speak out to known groups and not to amorphous and unfamiliar collections of people. In the case of the cursillo, Hervas and Bonnin did not undertake a revival of religion in general, but concentrated on a renewal within Christianity, and more particularly within Roman Catholicism. Clearly, they were primarily concerned with a select group within the church, an elite which was more easily converted to their program. They were not in pursuit of either ex-Catholics or nonpracticing members, but interested and believing Catholics. Hervas and Bonnin were never interested in preaching to the citizens of the world, but to a specific public whose values, norms, and religious problems they knew well before they began preaching the cursillo message.

The same factors seem to apply to other religious movements besides the cursillo. For example, Father Placide Tempels, the Belgian Franciscan missionary who began the jamaa, appealed to definite and restricted social groups. Tempels was not concerned with altering Catholicism as a whole, but addressed himself to the problems of African Roman Catholics residing in the general geographical area of Shaba and Kasai. Tempels possessed a vision, a dream, and it was directed specifically to the bearers of Catholic and Bantu ideologies.

In a similar vein, Mambu, the leader of a Melanesian cargo cult, addressed a definite audience; he appealed to the hopes, desires, and fears of the Kanaka people living in Tangu. It was Mambu's invocation of their past dreams, his intuitive interpretation of their cultural traditions and his presentation of an acceptable vision that generated and sustained his power.

It is in this sense that the work of charismatic leaders bears a similarity to the work of novelists and/or poets, since they are driven, in many instances, by the normative demands of their audience. The novelist and the poet write for particular social groups and are affected by the demands of these particular groups. As Sartre clearly knows:

> ... the author's choice of a certain aspect of the world determines the reader, and vice-versa, that it is by choosing his reader that the author decides upon his subject.
>
> Thus, all works of the mind contain within themselves the image of the reader for whom they are intended.[1]

Sartre is adamant in his belief that "one cannot write without a public,"[2] a public molded by certain historical and cultural factors that place restrictions and directives on the final work. There is a dialectical relationship between writers and their public and, similarly, between leaders and their followers. For just as the writer is shaped by his or her audience, the charismatic leader is influenced by the specific social groups addressed. Where there is charisma, there is the power of an audience conferring and acknowledging this force of leadership.

The charismatic leader is not one who stands apart from his or her public, but one who interacts with these followers. The charismatic leader faces a demanding audience that does not easily nor indiscriminately confer its authority. The leader receives power through performance; it is a performance marked by interaction and reaction. The leader employs words, but it is the interpretation of these words that effectuates the power of charisma. It is not the separation of leader and followers, but the intense relationship between them that generates the emergence of charisma.

There is one further, and quite interesting, similarity between charismatic leaders and writers. In the audience of each author, there is one person who has more weight in framing the textual work, one person who has more of an impact on the message than the rest of the audience. This person, sitting hypothetically in the audience of many writers, is none other than the author. Authors are engaged in a relation with themselves as they articulate the desires, visions, hopes, and fears of their social groups. Writers speak out to themselves, and because they are associated with these social groups and radically affected by them, their words have an impact on their audiences. Each author, if you will, participates in the ethos of his or her public, since each is a member of this very audience.

Juan Hervas and Edouardo Bonnin do address themselves. They are aware of their particular religious values and beliefs, as well as being cognizant of their personal frustrations and discontents with Catholicism.

Hervas specifically cites his membership and active engagement with Catholicism as significant in his assessment of the problems which besiege the church. He refers to a mutual struggle with Catholicism that affects him, and his followers, personally. Hervas is not removed from the difficulties troubling Catholicism, but is caught, as are other members of the church, in these very problems.

> Therefore for a priest—a man of God and of the Church—to be efficaciously a man of his time, he must know perfectly the reality on which he acts and he must use the most suitable means, even of the human order, to imbue this reality with the feeling of God.[3]

It is Hervas's personal frustrations with the direction of Catholicism and his belief in the church's inadequacies that impel his search for a method of renewal. It is Juan Hervas the individual, Juan Hervas the priest, who is searching, as much as his followers, for the desired alterations in the Catholic ideology.

In the case of Mambu, we find that he also articulates the vision of the new man for himself, as well as for the other Kanakas. Mambu and the people of Tangu are both upset by the unsettling effects of the European entrance into Melanesia. As the Kanakas pursue a satisfactory way of handling the ensuing social disturbances, Mambu is among the searchers. In Tangu, a cultural tradition is in the process of being shattered, and Mambu is not exempt from the impact of this cultural disintegration.

Mambu is both a leader and a follower. He articulates the fears and frustrations that he shares with the people of Tangu.

> Mambu is the first man we know about who tried, on a quasi-intellectual level, to relate the conclusions of his own experiences with white men to his Kanaka tradition.[4]

In confronting the problems of Tangu, Mambu confronts himself; in the words of Burridge, Mambu is "himself a

Analysis of the Movement

part of his own environment." As such, the dialogue of Mambu and his audience is first rooted in the monologue of Mambu and his self, for Mambu is his own leader first and second a leader of other Kanakas.

One may ask if the analogy breaks down in the case of Father Placide Tempels since he is a white Belgian missionary with followers who are black African Bantu. After spending years among the Bantu, Tempels emphatically believes one must learn to think and feel like an African if one is to understand and communicate successfully with this social group. As a reading of his *Bantu Philosophy* indicates, Tempels does in fact experience a symbolic conversion to African thought. Tempels thus addresses himself to the person he thinks he has become, namely, one with an understanding of the problems and dilemmas, as well as the spirit and dreams, of the Africans. In the words of Tempels:

> It is we who will be able to tell them, in precise terms, what their inmost concept of being is. They will recognize themselves in our words and will acquiesce, saying "You understand us: you now know us completely: you know in the way we know.[5]

The success of Tempels's message and the subsequent development of the jamaa movement testifies, in part, to his conversion to Bantu thought.

It is not assumed, however, that charismatic leaders always address themselves, but this phenomenon is more significant in the development of religious movements than is generally realized. Leaders must understand (as to stand under) their audiences, so that their articulations lead followers to an exciting and unparalleled conceptualization of themselves. In other words, by knowing their traditions and values, they can speak to their public in terms of these very experiences, allowing followers to make sense of their past. Leaders engineer this by making the problems and the crisis clear to them, using the tone and style that will create the greatest impact.

To be sure, all members of Hervas's and Bonnin's audience do not experience identical problems. But successful leaders can render their analyses in such an apt way that their followers perceive their own specific difficulties in the leaders' assessments and discover a personal solution in proposed programs. By deftly using analogies and metaphors, Hervas and Bonnin construct an interpretive paradigm which delineates and clarifies the religious problems of their public.

The important factor is not whether Hervas and Bonnin establish viewpoints that are objectively correct, but whether cursillistas concur with their articulations. From a scientific perspective, Hervas, for example, could be proven incorrect when he states:

> Here venerable brothers and beloved sons, you have the dark picture, the exact description of the actual world. . . . We can well, therefore, compare our age with the situation of the world at the historical moment of the barbarian invasions, or the times immediately preceding the coming of our divine Savior.[6]

Yet what is critical is Hervas's capacity to persuade individuals to support his perception of the world; that is, Hervas must convince others that his assessment of the social and religious situation is accurate. Kenneth Burke concurs that

> The subject of religion falls under the head of rhetoric in the sense that rhetoric is the art of

persuasion, and religious cosmologies are designed in the last analysis, as exceptionally thoroughgoing modes of persuasion.[7]

Hervas must not only succeed in outlining the problems of the past; he must also convince his audience that he possesses the answers for the present—a plan, a method, a message. He must assure others of the efficacy of his message, and this is what Hervas endeavors to accomplish. Consider, for example, the content and the style of the following passage:

> There is a conviction and state of soul which is spreading in all directions among men of good will who are persuaded that this is the age of Jesus, that "things cannot continue as they are," that this is the decisive hour, that the time has arrived for a return to a profounder Christianity, to a life of grace with deep consequences in every sphere of private and public life.
>
> A new world is surely being prepared, a new generation is rising with an interior eagerness to receive Christ. . . . Groups of priests and laymen are rising everywhere, animated with a generous, total and hierarchic self-giving, especially disposed to accept the greatest renunciation, to raise themselves to the loftiest heights of sanctity, in every state, office and profession.[8]

Here Hervas's plan is not depicted on a small-scale, but acknowledged as a method with the potential to renew the world. His plan focuses on the self, the family, and the environment, impressing members with a powerful vision of the future.

To be sure, Hervas and Bonnin as charismatic leaders possess special abilities, but as previously stated, these abilities do not stem from mystical forces. If Juan Hervas and Edouardo Bonnin are extraordinary, they are so as good poets, playwrights, and novelists are unusual. What makes these individuals extraordinary is their phenomenal ability to create forcefully and to impress deeply. In their messages, whether it be within the poem, the play, or the charismatic plan, they are able to transform their audiences' personal and social perspectives.

Hervas and Bonnin are extraordinary in their acute perceptions of the frustrations facing Catholics and their unusual skills in devising an acceptable solution. These men are not only perceptive, they are also extremely articulate and capable of presenting their message clearly and forcefully. Hervas and Bonnin possess an understanding of their public, and they are able to give voice to these feelings. Clearly, charismatic leaders cannot remain mute. Their silence must be transcended. The major documents and minor publications attest to Hervas's role as a prolific commentator on the cursillo ideology. These texts reveal his awareness of his role as a formulator and articulator.

According to Hervas, language must be "alive, modern and comprehensible" since today's audiences "detest what is florid [and] baroque."[9] He comprehends the consequence of language in the success of a movement, asserting that:

> Images and comparisons are very effective, when used moderately; let the syntax be simple, the language modern, using if possible, the language of the listeners in its more noble and elevated terms.[10]

Charismatic leaders then are creative, intuitive individuals who have a following because they understand their audience and because they can offer perceptive messages that make sense in light of their experiences and can conjure excitement. They present a reenactment of a dream, a picture of what is and a world of what can be. Thus Burridge's description of Mambu applies to Hervas and Bonnin where each is:

> A rebel, a radical, a man sufficiently able to free himself from the circumstances of his time to grasp what he thought to be valuable in tradition and weld it to his perception of what he would have liked the future to be.[11]

Hervas and Bonnin are radical for they share the artist's desire and drive to invent and create. They are radical because they are not satisfied with the church's designs for living and depart from the strict traditional approach in forging a different paradigm. As leaders, these two men are innovators who propose, within a religious framework, a process of renewal. We can say that Hervas and Bonnin are driven men, but not in an abnormal sense. They are driven in their desire to create again, to renew, and to persuade. They use the past, and as they do, Hervas and Bonnin uncover meanings captured in early Christianity. What was formerly static and lifeless becomes dynamic and exciting, as these cursillo leaders endeavor to make religion and culture a process once again.

The rebelliousness of Hervas and Bonnin is a phase of innovation, and their radicalness arises from their departure from the expected pattern of Catholic behavior. Using their knowledge of the past, they are not bound by it, but accept the challenge to deviate in order to create. Employing themes and images that are already present in their religious tradition, they generate a different religious world view. It is an image of themselves and of their audience; it is a vision of the new person.

Just as the poet is aware of the collapse of meaning and the rigidity of language, Hervas and Bonnin are conscious of what George Steiner calls "verbal inflation," where more and more words are needed to convey understanding. Hervas and Bonnin both attack what can be called the baroque quality of Catholicism; they focus on the antiquarian images and the "patching" of metaphors. Both men experience a discontent with the meaninglessness of the church's traditional approach. Their discontent, however, is not normal but expected, when values and beliefs no longer provide men and women with a rich reservoir of meaning. It is a discontent with religious language that has become rigid and ineffectual; where metaphors collapse, and analogies are worn thin; and language is not pushed to its frontier, but remains stagnant and becomes a cliche. It is this linguisitc situation that Hervas and Bonnin battle, laboring to invigorate and enliven Catholicism. For Hervas and Bonnin, this entails the creation of meaning and excitement, giving Christianity a rich and expressive language.

The problem of legitimation, however, is not resolved with charisma. Just as writers are not split from their literary tradition, charismatic leaders are not separated from theirs. Charisma is important, but it is not the only means of legitimating the cursillo. Although some social scientists opt for a choice between charisma and tradition, the dichotomization of these two processes is inappropriate when analyzing the cursillo. In this movement, charisma and tradition are intertwined, and legitimation requires both the creative and critical abilities of Hervas and Bonnin, and the realm of Catholic tradition.

There are probably few religious movements where

Analysis of the Movement

charisma does not embrace some degree of tradition. The careers of charismatic leaders as Yali, Mambu, and Simon Kimbangu, for example, vindicate the importance of holding a position, office, or kin alignment that is respected and honored by one's potential audience. Prior to their association with any movement, these men already possessed a potential source of power. They all held positions which provided them with an available audience of individuals who were inclined to listen. These men were able to successfully take advantage of their situation, yet their capacity to do so appears to be significantly rooted in the particular social positions they maintained.

Utilizing an authorized position within the Catholic hierarchy is not limited to the cursillo, as the jamaa, Lutherism, and the Thomas Muntzer[12] and Father Cicero[13] movements reveal. It is not accidental that these men—Luther, Thomas Muntzer, Father Cicero, and Tempels—at some point in their lives are Roman Catholic priests, and that the latter two remain so. All four men were recognized, for a time, as legitimate interpreters of Catholic doctrine, and as acknowledged preachers. Their consecration as priests predisposed Catholic followers to believe in their message.

Hervas was not only an ordained priest but also a consecrated bishop. Therefore he had considerable channels of legitimation at his disposal. He could preach, instruct, and innovate. Not only was this acceptable; it was expected. Hervas does not refrain from employing his position to affirm the efficacy and judiciousness of the cursillo, but defends his traditional power:

> My sixty years of human experience, my thirty-two years as a priest and eighteen years as a Bishop authorize me to make this statement.[14]

Charisma and Tradition

Hervas frequently emphasizes his roles and responsibilities within the traditional hierarchy and when necessary wields his position as a source of persuasion. When his statements cannot be adequately proven, he resorts to his experiences as a priest and as a bishop:

> If the explanation does not turn out to be sufficient proof for the reader, at least let him accept the convinced testimony of an old pastor of souls who traveled over the world studying apostolic movements, who has directed apostolic associations, and who little by little, by a special Grace of God has gone deeply and joyously into the meaning of the Church's liturgical movement.[15]

At times, Hervas merges both tradition and charisma as he attempts to get followers to support his interpretive paradigm.

> I think that my answer merits acceptance because of the responsibility that is mine and for the part I have taken in the beginning, development and present state of the work of the Cursillos in Christianity.[16]

Hervas is aware that his voice as bishop and founder, although powerful, is not sufficient to impress his audience of the judiciousness of his message. To increase his credibility, he relies on the added voices of other members of the Roman Catholic hierarchy. Hervas, perhaps even more than Bonnin, is conscious of the problem of legitimation, and thus actively searches for supporters:

> I realize that the affirmation of an individual is not sufficient to awaken the reader's curiosity, nor to convince him of the extreme importance

> of the subject I am writing about . . . I think the best thing to do is to bring before the reader a procession of trustworthy characters, each of whom will give evidence. These witnesses will be Cardinals, Archbishops, Bishops, priests, religious and laymen.[17]

In this particular text Hervas presents eleven pages of testimonies from members of the Catholic church who describe the impact of the cursillo on their lives or within their dioceses. Significantly, these testimonies are not those of anonymous or inconsequential Catholics, but known, respected, and authorized voices of the church. As such, these testimonies delineate the success of the cursillo in attaining a renewal, but they also serve to securely place the cursillo within the legitimate realm of the Catholic Church. The words of one bishop exemplifies this point:

> The first thing to be said—clearly—is that the Cursillo movement is a movement of the Church, in the Church and for the Church.[18]

The endorsements vary in the words and expressions used, yet they all serve to affirm a similar feeling, namely, enthusiasm, respect, and credibility for the cursillo. One American bishop declares:

> The Little Courses (cursillo) have occasioned a wonderful movement of grace in this diocese from the beginning.
>
> We know that the Cursillo movement rests theologically on the solidity of its doctrine centered in the life of grace lived in the Mystical Body of Christ. . . .
>
> We have given the movement our blessing in

Charisma and Tradition

the past and gladly call down God's renewed blessing upon it.[19]

In a similar fashion, an archbishop reveals:

> We know from personal experience . . . the great importance of the Cursillo Movement. It is a providential instrument for the formation of true Christian leaders. Cursillo is a movement, not an organization. Through its inner dynamism, we have witnessed effective and lasting leadership training for parishes and apostolic units.[20]

The repeated use of these and other testimonies indicates Hervas's awareness of their critical role in the success of the cursillo. Because he was a bishop, Hervas's testimony was consequential but because he was also one of the founders of the movement, he needed other voices not associated with the founding efforts to vouch for the program's legitimacy. Finding archbishops, bishops, and priests sincerely impressed with the cursillo, Hervas uses their words. Even when these statements appear as simple wishes of success, they serve to endorse the cursillo as an acceptable, fruitful, and legitimate Catholic movement.

In addition to testimonies, Hervas also employs church documents to justify the cursillo framework. In his texts, he juxtaposes particular documented statements with certain cursillo ideas or procedures. In such instances, he persuades his audience of the cursillo's faithfulness to Catholic beliefs. The cursillo texts refer to papal statements, particularly those of Pius XII who reigned during the formative years of the movement, and these are also used to convince readers that the cursillo is fulfilling the papal mandate of Christian renewal.

Analysis of the Movement

It is interesting to note that Hervas imputes an equal significance to all the papal statements reprinted in his texts, giving the impression that these papal statements are generally encyclical material. Yet many statements stem from rather insignificant addresses, as the blessing of a cornerstone of the Spanish Pontifical College (October 13, 1956), or a papal address to the International Federation of Catholic Men (December 8, 1956). In effect, Hervas uses any papal statement which can profit the legitimation of the cursillo. Hervas's research on papal documents at the University of Freidburg, provided him with the knowledge he skillfully employs to successfully align certain papal statements with cursillo beliefs and methodology. When these statements are put in the context of the cursillo documents, the implication is papal approval for the theoretical and doctrinal basis of the movement. These papal pronouncements, as presented by Hervas, serve as "proof" that the cursillo is fulfilling the sanctioned wish of the church.

Hervas does not falsely record the words of various popes. However, by taking phrases and paragraphs out of context, the original meanings are dramatically altered. Once these statements are removed from their context, various interpretations are easily implied. Surely Pius XII had, at one time or another, mentioned the necessity of Christian renewal; however, he never called for the creation and expansion of the cursillo movement.

Thus, the legitimation of the cursillo is intricate and complex. It is not a simple case of charisma, nor the obvious use of tradition, but a careful and innovative weaving of both. In the cursillo, charisma and Catholic tradition are creatively interrelated to provide a viable legitimation of the cursillo. Charisma, then, as part of the process of legtimation and part of the creation and expansion of a movement necessitates the dimension of work. Not to see this is to too easily reduce charisma to a psychological dimension instead of focusing on the dynamic transactions within an interacting situation. Likewise, it is to not understand that legitimation also entails the work of integrating tradition within the movement. It is in the relation of the work of charisma to the work of tradition that the cursillo expands beyond the confines of Mallorca to become an international movement, increasing in numbers from the few in the 1940s to almost two million today.

Charisma does not end with Hervas and Bonnin, nor is it limited to Mallorca and Cuidad Real, but continues to mark the cursillo in the actions of certain spiritual directors. In some locations and for many individuals, there is no charisma, only tradition and the established cursillo roles. But in certain areas, the expansion of the movement and the number and depth of committed members is related to the presence of an unusual person, a spiritual director whose interactions are marked by charismatic qualities.

At Ocean Bay, more is heard about Fr. Greg Brovane than is heard about Hervas or Bonnin. To these members, he is "Father Cursillo." If Hervas and Bonnin are well known, it is because Father Brovane emphasizes the early founders' texts and attempts to closely abide with their structure. At Ocean Bay the force and shaping influence has been his. The success of the movement, in terms of numbers, organization, and degree of commitment is tied to Father Brovane's dynamic and powerful impact. As members frequently remark:

> He has been a gift. He is a very special person. He has time for those in the highest office, the

Analysis of the Movement

> boards, the rectors and those who live the Fourth Day. The concern is the same; his love is the same.

> He takes the simplest things and makes of them a ceremony. He is able to point out the Christ-like moments in our days. He brings awareness of this to us. If there is a problem he shows it as a blessing and how it may be good.

> His special gift is that he brings out a lot in people. He finds something that someone can give: he finds their gift. It can be their sensitivity, their kindness—it doesn't have to be talent or writing. Everyone has special gifts. He is able to remember everyone's name and does not forget these gifts that he has seen in people.

Father Brovane grasps aspects of people that others do not perceive, that even they themselves are not clear about. He gives back to members an image of themselves so that they may know the person that they are. His ability is to tap their talents, to understand them better than they know themselves; he becomes a mirror to some unrecognized aspect of themselves. This extraordinary ability is potentially present in human interaction. Some never seem to tap this human resource, other are unsuccessful in their attempts, while a few, like Father Brovane, are masters.

There is another aspect to Father Brovane's persuasive powers, which is illuminated in this team leader's words: "He has always had a vision." As he himself openly admits:

> I am very affected by the idea that we have a dream and a vision; then we sense the woundedness of our humanity and third, reality sets in.

Charisma and Tradition

People are at all stages in the cursillo and we need all three. In the second stage we lose a lot, but we human beings are wounded. Some get to feel that there is more and get to the next stage where they can celebrate life.

There is a wholesomeness in the cursillo. It respects the basic humanness of people and brings life to its wholesomeness. Holiness is wholesome.

All Jesus wants is for us to find our humanness, to be fully alive. Our humanness is a gift and so is the growth of community. To celebrate life is important.

There has been room in the cursillo for people with vision since its beginning, from the early plan for the monumental pilgrimage to St. John Compostela to the later, dynamic perspective of life itself as a pilgrimage. Within the contours of charisma lies the power of a vibrant vision.

Maybe we have always been unclear about charisma. Perhaps we have not understood that the prophet never was a magician, that he never pulled anything from the hat, but always worked with what was there and with the people in his midst. Perhaps we have too often fallen into the fallacy of thinking that charisma is an all-or-nothing phenomenon. Assuming this, some researchers have characterized certain people as charismatic, while others were seen as separate from its force. Yet what we are discussing is the human potential to affect the very foundation of what it means to be human: to touch and influence people in the very act of interacting with them. Charisma involves the ability to forge dreams, to kindle desires, and to make life alive and vibrant, or at least to promise this human dream to men and women.

Analysis of the Movement

Perhaps in some situations, for a very short time, we all have touched charisma, but we could not sustain it. We all act and instill responses in others; some do this with an extra intensity and a force that lives longer than their immediate presence. We hear; some make us listen. We walk; some make us dance. Charisma is the ability to go beyond oneself, bringing others to praxis and to their sense of destiny. For each of us, in being human, the future is open and holds the potential for change. The charismatic individual brings forth the human vision so that others may be drawn toward their own fulfillment. Not regardless of culture and history, but because of both, human beings come to know the possibility of becoming and the sense of themselves as open to time. In a significant way, the charismatic individual affects the humanness of men and women, making that very dimension alive and exciting. The deeper meaning that underlies religious salvation is the rescue from alienation and the rescue of past images as they fuse in the dreams of the future; it involves giving back to people their ability to create new images and new worlds.

Notes

1. J. Sartre, *What is Literature?*, trans B. Frechtman (New York: Washington Square Press, 1966), p. 45.

2. Ibid., p. 101.

3. J. Hervas, "The 'Cursillos de Christiandad' (Part II)," *Christ to the World* 2 (1962): 322.

4. K. Burridge, "Cargo Cult Activity in Tangu," *Oceania* 24 (1954): 177–78.

5. P. Tempels, *Bantu Philosphy* (Paris: Présence Africaine, 1959), p. 36.

6. J. Hervas, *Cursillos in Christianity—Instrument of Christian Renewal*, trans. W. Young (Phoenix: Ultreya Press, 1965), p. 28.

7. K. Burke, *The Rhetoric of Religion: Studies in Logology* (Berkeley: University of California Press, 1970), p. v.

8. Hervas, *Instrument of Renewal*, p. 31.

9. Ibid., p. 318.

10. Ibid.

11. K. Burridge, *Mambo: A Study of Melanesian Cargo Movements and their Social and Ideological Background* (New York: Harper and Row, 1970), p. xv.

12. N. Cohn, "Medieval Millenarism: Its Bearing on the Comparative Study of Millenarian Movements" in *Millenial Dreams in Action*, ed. S. Thrupp (The Hague: Mouton, 1962).

Analysis of the Movement

13. Ribeiro, R. "Brazilian Messianic Movements" in *Millenial Dreams in Action,* ed. S. Thrupp (The Hague: Mouton, 1962).

14. J. Hervas, "The 'Cursillos de Christiandad' (Part I)," *Christ to the World 2* (1962): 167.

15. J. Hervas, *Questions and Problems Concerning Cursillos in Christianity,* trans. W. Young (Phoenix: Ultreya Press, 1966), p. 51.

16. Ibid., p. 274.

17. J. Hervas, "The 'Cursillos De Christiandad' (Part I)," *Christ to the World 2* (1962): 167.

18. Ibid., p. 169.

19. Hervas, *Instrument of Renewal,* p. 13.

20. J. Capo, *The Group Reunion,* trans. J. Brown (Phoenix: Ultreya Press, 1969), p. 2.

CHAPTER 8

THE LANGUAGE OF A MOVEMENT: ON SPEAKING CURSILLO

Analysis of the Movement

Years ago Heidegger wrote:

> Language is not a mere tool that man possesses in addition to many others; on the contrary, it is only language that affords man the very possibility of standing in the openness of Being. Only where there is language is there a world.[1]

Only where there is language can the cursillo exist as a movement, for it is through speech and texts that a world is formed, maintained, and passed on to others. It is through language that the cursillo grapples with the problems affecting traditional Catholicism, and through language it offers alternatives to action and thought. Language is not merely, or even most significantly, a system for telling others what a phenomenon is about; centrally, language is the symbolic system through which a phenomenon comes to be and its social reality is expressed. It is in this sense that the speech of the cursillo becomes central to an investigation of the movement. Heidegger also understood that words have been given to men and women that they may come to know Being.[2] One could likewise say that language has been given to the cursillistas in order that they may testify to who they are—socially, spiritually, ontologically.

In the cursillo there is an emphasis on using different terms and expressing Christian dogma in new phrases. Attention is openly paid to communication. Does this mean, some may ask, that members are aware of Heidegger's stance? Does it imply that members of the cursillo fully comprehend this linguistic dimension for themselves and for others? Generally the answer is that they do not. This is to be expected when we consider another aspect of language, namely, that it shapes an individual's world and being, without any necessary realiza-

The Language of a Movement

tion of this process. In this way, the most significant feature of language can appear as the least significant when words are being spoken. The power of language rests in masking its utter powerfulness; so that we generally see language as instrumental and not as expressive of our own social reality. In other words, the ontological and metalinguistic dimensions of language do not generally surface in everyday usage. For although language provides and shapes the experience of the world, individuals do not usually experience the experience of language within them.

It is for this reason that descriptions of what the cursillo does with speech are not enough. We are not solely concerned with the understanding members have of their language; we need to know more. For this we need to analyze and delve into the sphere of language and to wrestle with areas that may not be understood by the very members who speak the language of the cursillo. Here again, we confront the differences between discussions of the cursillo by members and the presentation of the cursillo by a social scientist. The former deals with a telling of what has occurred; the latter with uncovering and analyzing what is neither obvious nor always publicly acknowledged.

Derrida knowingly wrote:

> It remains, then, for us to *speak,* to make our voices *resonate* throughout the corridors in order to make up for the breakup of presence.[3]

There is no doubt that this sense of speaking is central to the cursillo; it is the mode of being, part of the rite of passage and the very work of the movement. It is central to the tripod image of action as witness and sharing, piety as responding to God, and study as communicating to oneself and others one's observations of the world. Even the follow-up meetings of the group reunions and the ultreyas are established to guarantee a continuation of the "sense of speaking," as individuals give voice to others about their failures and their successes. For here it is speech that is redemptive and liberating.

The words of this speech will not always be familiar, due to the cursillo's need to claim new links and to provide meanings not called forth in older traditional terms. Thus carved from myriad sounds, the words—palanca, rollo, ultreya, de colores, and cursillo—are spoken. Foreign terms, purposefully kept untranslatable, call forth the ideas and methodology of this movement. This is because, as Derrida clearly saw, "unheard-of thoughts are required, sought for across the memory of old signs."[4] There is an essentialness grasped in these terms; these newer sounds give voice to changed perceptions and more vivid images.

In the cursillo, it is not just a talk that is given; it is a rollo demanding witnessing and sharing. Palanca, likewise, are not just traditional renunciations, but sacrifices shared with others; not private actions, but publicly disclosed intentions—that is palanca. Similarly, the cursillo is not just a short course in Christianity: it is a movement, a way of life. It is cursillo.

Yet not all terms used in the cursillo are new; older terms are still significant. However, this should not lead us to the assumption that their meaning is necessarily traditional. Clearly, they are not. Words, such as Christ, Jesus, love, Christianity, community, and prayer are marked with an "invisible sedimentation"[5] of traditional Catholicism which the cursillo struggles to dislodge. Thus the cursillo goes beyond the older interpretive layers, to a different historical time—to early Christianity.

The Language of a Movement

We can say that the cursillo "labors always to restore a *primordial* sense to these terms, a *sense* which *began* to be perverted at the time of its inscription into the tradition"⁶ of its historical roots.

There is, then, a definite attempt to rekindle many terms with the meaning found in early Christianity, and as Hervas himself writes:

> Return to primitive Christianity should mean the return to the spirit which animated the actions and conduct characteristic of the life of those fervent Christians: life which is all light, spirit and warmth . . . in the bosom of a family, a community, where everything spoke of the unity of God and the fraternity of men. Life which developed around the Apostles, hearing the divine Word from their lips, who bore witness to all they had seen, heard and touched.⁷

So, familiar terms are employed, but their meanings are not always conventional, given the intention of conveying meanings not generally associated with these Catholic phrases. In this way, cursillistas incorporate words that traditional Catholics also use, but there are times this perceived similarity is deceptive. The meaning of their words rests in the new grammar of the cursillo, which both introduces new terms and employs older ones charged with unexpected interpretations.

From its beginnings in Mallorca, the cursillo has grasped the power of language. Hervas and Bonnin both recognize the forcefulness of language; its ability to seize followers. Both understand the impact of language in altering the perceptions and perspectives of their audience. Yet both Hervas and Bonnin are not satisfied with ephemeral changes, for their goal demands total conversion to

Analysis of the Movement

the cursillo, where each day is guided by piety, study, and action.

Hervas specifically searches for a way to convey simply, yet forcefully, the cursillo perspective. He desires a technique which compresses cursillo ideology without reducing the impact of its message. Hervas searches for words that dispatch the power to evoke strong emotional responses and that can engender joy, optimism, and determination. Aware of the role of sayings like "God wills it" during the Crusades, he labors to formulate comparable phrases for the cursillo. In this way, mottos become central to the movement.

Within the genre of the motto, the phrase that is the most successful and most integrated into the members' linguistic world is the phrase de colores. In Spanish these words refer to colors, a signification that marks the cursillo. As a motto, de colores reminds members of the rainbow; the various colors merge into one phenomenon, representing the very brotherhood and sisterhood of the movement. Moreover, it conjures up the excitement and élan of initiation where this phrase is first heard; it is also a reminder of group reunions and ultreyas, where it is continually used. When members greet each other, they embrace heartily and one warmly conveys "de colores." In response, the other echoes back the often-repeated words, "de colores." This is generally communicated with spirit and emotion, it is not casual. Stated with deliberation and enthusiasm, de colores is exchanged with an intensity that, if it cannot be statistically measured, can certainly be observed. After the embrace, individuals gaze at each other and exchange smiles and good wishes. As a greeting, it is not typically American, but this unusual mode of interaction soon becomes part of

The Language of a Movement

the members' way of life. The handshake gives way to the embrace, for it is not so much two Americans who are meeting, but two individuals each sharing and expressing the message of the cursillo. The de colores embrace symbolizes and embodies the spirit of the movement in terms of caring, action, piety, and community. It is this that is affirmed in the embrace and this that is made evident in the concrete exchange of these particular words.

More than a phrase, de colores is the symbolic expression of the movement. Like the clenched fist of earlier political movements, it echoes the ideals, the goals, and the actual living of the movement. In many ways, de colores attests to the power of language to constitute a social reality in the very process of expressing an ideal. It is as if flashbacks of significant cursillo images, events, and interactions are brought into focus when de colores is spoken. For this reason, there is no other phrase that testifies so much to a person's being a cursillista than the voicing of this particular phrase. De colores becomes symbolic of the Christian community which exchanges it.

It would be a mistake, however, to think that de colores is only communicated verbally or when individuals meet. This phrase is also evident in written forms of communication. In writing to one another and especially in palancas, members convey de colores. It begins and ends communication and serves as a warm greeting to cursillistas. Individuals also create and buy plaques decorated with this saying. In many homes, these wooden pieces are hung on the walls, symbolizing to members and visitors the influence cursillo effects upon their family and social life. The most public display of this phrase is observed in the decision to place decals on the bumpers or back windows of automobiles. In a society where people travel by

Analysis of the Movement

cars, leaving walking and its accompanying face-to-face exchanges to a minimum, de colores decals serve to greet, in the spirit of the cursillo, the cursillistas they pass by.

Although it is the most significant phrase, de colores is not the only motto in the cursillo; within the movement there are a variety of phrases that can be grouped into two distinct categories. The first comprises those mottos found in most cursillo groups, regardless of ethnic, regional, or cultural factors. They are the standardized maxims of the movement, the generic category. The second category, here termed parochial, embraces those mottos that formulate cursillo ideas in the particular idioms of the various regional groups, reflecting the divergent styles and tones within the cursillo membership. Given that the parochial mottos are specific to each area, we would not expect these to surface outside the Ocean Bay area.

De colores exemplifies the type of phrase contained within the generic category; in interviews with cursillistas from Lansing, Chicago, Boston, Ponta Delgada (Azores), and Ocean Bay, this phrase consistently symbolized the essence of the cursillo program. As a phrase, it is expressed and exchanged regardless of geographic differences. One reason why generic mottos are present in spite of cultural and regional differences is the interweaving of these maxims with the main themes and beliefs of the cursillo. As the movement expanded from Mallorca and Ciudad Real, many of these mottos were associated with specific cursillo beliefs and techniques. A second factor which rooted the generic mottos within each region is their inscription in the major cursillo texts. By being printed in Hervas's documents, the generic mottos were assured a degree of permanence and importance. Since these texts are required reading for

The Language of a Movement

members, studying these documents occasions a simultaneous exposure to the mottos.

The following mottos exemplify the generic classification:

1. Christ and I, an overwhelming majority.
2. It is not enough to live in grace; we must live grace.
3. Don't waste your time reading good books; read only the best.
4. Christ is counting on you.
5. A sad saint is a sorry saint.
6. Contact with Christ and with the brothers.
7. For the Apostle, one hour of study is an hour of prayer.
8. Don't judge perfection by its cost, but by what it is worth.
9. The fault is not always of the wicked, but of the good who could be better.
10. Without me you can do nothing.
11. Do it because it costs and precisely because it costs.

Certain phrases in the generic group may vary from one group to another; but when they differ, the alterations are slight, with changes entailing minor variations in phraseology. Consider, for example, the following phrases from Ocean Bay and Chicago which could be substituted without altering the basic meaning of the motto:

Analysis of the Movement

12. (a) Study is action taking aim.
    (b) Study is the marksmanship of action.
13. (a) We are not saved nor are we condemned alone, but in groups.
    (b) We shall not save ourselves nor condemn ourselves alone, but in clusters.
14. (a) Sons of the Father, brothers of Christ, temples of the Holy Spirit, heirs of Heaven.
    (b) Sons of the Father, brothers of Christ, temples of the Holy Spirit.

Directly and indirectly, the generic mottos affirm the basic techniques of piety, study, or action, as well as revealing the focus of self, family, or environment. For example, the idea of brotherhood and sisterhood, so central to the cursillo, is signified in the motto, "We are not saved nor are we condemned alone, but in groups." Here the word *group* does not refer to any general social gathering of Christians, but to the particular group reunions and the ultreyas. Its message is Christianity lived with and through others, with specific reference to the communal nature of Christianity enacted and represented in the postcursillo meetings.

Similarly, the phrase "A sad saint is a sorry saint" opposes a cheerless and spiritless Christianity, upholding the need to express a hopeful response in one's daily life. Religion from this perspective evolves from love, not fear. Given the importance of saintliness, and the emphasis on grace, cursillistas apprehend that they are not to reach this state through sorrow, but through joy. That one can be saved by smiling instead of crying, through rejoicing instead of suffering, is this motto's message. Sacrifice is not abandoned, but rethought to include the cheerful giving of oneself to others. Thus holiness emerges in friendship, by partaking together in a heartwarming Christian community; an open and spirited giving of oneself is asked, smiles and not tears. The motto affirms the smile as an essential human expression; animals do not smile, but individuals can reveal their inner selves to one another in this symbolic display of their humanity. It is this that is encouraged in choosing cheerfulness over sadness.

"For the Apostle, one hour of study is an hour of prayer." Traditionally Catholic hermeneutics was, for the most part, relegated to the clergy. It was assumed that priests, trained in analyzing theological texts, should be the interpreters of these religious subjects. Unlike other Christian denominations that designated a wide circle of interpreters, Catholics have not generally upheld such an orientation. However, this phrase affirms a new direction, launching a task that demands reading and study of religious texts, and thereby placing a greater responsibility on members to take an active and critical role.

But there is more; the motto situates study on a level with piety, thereby asserting a connection that is not always realized, namely, that reflection is related to prayer. It makes reading and scholarly work that many once relegated to a secular realm part of member's religious activity. It reestablishes reading and study as part of each member's responsibility, generating a more active and reflective membership.

"Christ and I, an overwhelming majority," proclaims the significant union between members and Christ, yet it is a different relationship than previously experienced. For here, "Christ and I" affirms a relationship of friendship, pointing to the image of Christ as friend. Unlike the older notion of Christ as Father, a figure of awe and fear, here Christ is visualized as a brother. Christ is understood as a Being with whom each person can communicate and one on whom each can rely. His divinity is still present, but he is not conceptualized as a frightening figure. The humanity of Christ is brought in balance; previously the stress on his divinity left many with an image that was incompatible with a joyful communication. Christ of the cursillo is human and divine; the fact that Christ was made man is never forgotten.

"Contact with Christ and with the brothers" encourages members to communicate with Christ. "Contact with Christ" is the overwhelming message—not avoidance or fear of communication. Christ is seen as approachable and knowing this, members are encouraged to seek Christ out. Contact with Christ also grounds contact with other cursillistas; not the solitary life, nor the isolation of praying alone, but action with others is the objective. Contact with the brothers is necessarily contact with Christ.

"Without Me you can do nothing" emphatically acknowledges the need for Christ in the member's lives and clearly speaks to the creative power that underlies the world. In the cursillo another dimension besides culture and human invention allows the human powers to flourish and exist, Christ. In the movement it is to Christ that members give thanks for their talents and accomplishments. In this way, this motto asserts that Christ is a necessary part of their mundane existence.

The generic mottos disclose the continual affirmation of Christ in the lives of members. When old answers fade and wither, people go in search of new ones. In the cursillo, "Christ is the answer" to the many essential questions of life. Yes, there are numerous questions, yet the resolution for cursillistas comes to completion in Christ.

The Language of a Movement

First, this means the idea of a personal relationship with Christ, where Christ is not distant and removed, but is an immediate and forceful manifestation in their everyday lives. For some this presence is so overwhelming that it is as if every cell is drenched in the reality of Christ. This experience is a sharp contrast for many who previously held only a belief in Christ, for it was exactly that—a tenet of faith, an intellectual position. For many, there is a radical shift that is caught in this motto, "In the cursillo the truth enters into the head and explodes in the heart." The "explosion" catches people off-guard; they are overwhelmed by the *experience* of Christ. "Christ is there with you"; for this woman, the sense of her soul became alive and meaningful as she experienced Christ within her. An idea that had previously been trite, vague, and inconsequential in her life, now became dominant and vibrant. Another person disclosed the experience of Christ in this way:

> It was a very personal experience. I had had an intellectual approach and was heady of faith. I had lost the capacity to feel. It simplified the message of what Christianity is all about.

Cursillistas thus acquire a "faith experience" in the personal encounter of Christ.

Second, it means that Christ is the ideal, the typification for their lives. He provides the model, "He brings God's vision for man." Here the conception of a model comprises none other than an ontological dimension. It is "God's vision," a conception of human destiny that goes beyond logic and reason, a humanness shaped by a theological design. The sense of becoming and of process directed by a divine goal is felt; it is the very possibility of a religiously defined praxis. In this way, the experience of

Analysis of the Movement

Christ is directly linked to the experience of being human. It is as if men and women become spiritual images; sensing their incompleteness, they search for perfection according to a metaphysical plan that entails an ontological project.

Third, taking Christ as their answer ushers forth a triumphant, optimistic attitude. Consider again the motto "Christ and I, an overwhelming majority." We can see that members maintain their ability to achieve their goals and to carry out Christian actions. The personal experience of Christ affirms that, in the fourth day, they are different, and being with Christ, transformations of environments are possible. The *work* of renewal is joyful, optimistic, and geared to new objectives. The involvement of self in community is directed and inspired by a restored spirituality: it becomes a spiritual praxis in search of a world.

Clearly, joy is part of the cursillo. "A Christian has a right to be enthusiastic" reaffirms this dimension where rejoicing and happiness are encouraged. It is the resurrected Christ—the Christ of Easter—that is the Christ of the cursillo. The Christ of the cross and of the passion is necessary, but is not as emphasized as the Divinity which symbolizes afterlife and resurrection to its members.

Fourth, we can speak of the Christianization of the world which demands a shift in values for cursillistas. The answer, then, is to become a new person, to be reborn with distinguishing priorities, with a new heart whose center is not oneself but Christ. What this means is to be a daughter, to be a son, accepting divinity as a gift and as a vital presence in one's life. The reality of self, world, and of God is altered, and its impact is felt in the transformation of the initiates; candidates become the

The Language of a Movement

"cutting edge of Christianity" and their very essence is overwhelmingly affected.

Fifth, this encompasses the living community, bonded together in the belief that Christ is central, that He is brother to all people, and that He is the vital link between men and women. It necessitates sharing one's faith with others and moving from a solitary to a more public, communal faith. In the cursillo, members are encouraged to "Spread the word and share it."

In a society where many issues are unclear and where answers are felt to be tenuous and equivocal, "Christ is the answer" becomes a powerful, lived solution for cursillistas.

While generic mottos proclaim the main themes and orientations of the cursillo, the parochial mottos profess the need of each specific cursillo group to draft ideas in their own style and in their own idiom. Remember that the cursillo began because traditional Catholicism did not speak the language of its people. For this reason, the cursillo has from its beginning tried to be meaningful to people living in today's world and to capture the pulse of its members.

It is part of the process of language that individuals are always contributing to their understanding of the movement by introducing new analogies and expressions. Eliot's lines:

> Words strain,
> Crack and sometimes break, under the burden,
> Under the tension, slip, slide, perish,
> Decay with imprecision, will not stay in place,
> Will not stay still[8]

not only capture a poetic expression, but reveal an insightful philosophical position. Language is a process that can effect a transformation; speech is altered in the very process of affecting people's sense of the world. Eliot has grasped the dialectic lodged in the anthropological position that "language uses us as much as we use it." Language transforms and is itself reshaped in the process of communication.

The parochial mottos arise from the daily expressions in general use within the various geographical regions, including advertising jingles and slang expressions. Since expressions currently in fashion distinguish this grouping, it is not surprising that this category will undergo more changes than the generic mottos.

The following mottos exemplify the parochial category:

1. We share in the ongoingness of our salvation.
2. To attain an ideal, you've got to be you.
3. Make Christ real in your life.
4. Jesus is where the action is.
5. Actual grace is a now presence, a now sharing, a now gift.
6. Sin is a contradiction of what love is all about.
7. Through grace we become Spirit people, Christ people.
8. Sin is a reality that cramps our style.
9. If you live in fear of God, you may as well forget it.
10. Don't keep the faith, spread it.

The Language of a Movement

11. Let God mind your business.
12. Life is like a dance with free movement and self-expression.
13. Accentuate the positive.
14. We are part of His Master plan.
15. It's a joy to be a true Christian.

"Make Christ real in your life" directs individuals to change their view that Christ was basically a historical figure living among farmers and fishermen to see him as a dynamic and commanding figure relevant to twentieth century thought. It is a Christ who is concerned with the problems of present-day men and women.

It is not surprising to discover many mottos using the words *real* and *reality,* since these terms are frequently used in advertisements and in present-day conversations. Consider, for example, "Sin is a reality that cramps our style." Here, sin is depicted as an ever-present phenomenon which limits a person's full potential. Sin should be avoided, not because it is a "black spot" on one's soul, but because it impedes ongoing Christian action. Sin hampers goodness and restricts love, and for this reason members should avoid it. Unlike the traditional definition of sin as committing negative acts, the cursillo presents sin as insufficient love. Sin is not so much a condition of evil, as it is not performing enough good.

"To attain an ideal, you've got to be you," reflects the idea of being oneself, frequently emphasized in commercials, publications, and songs. Yet the focus here is on the need for members to know themselves, to critically reflect on who they are, and to give witness to that very dimension. Their goal is not to become someone other than themselves, but to arrive at their spiritual center. It endorses meditation and self-reflection to actualize the objectives of piety, study, and action. In this way, individuals may grasp the breadth of their importance to their family, to the movement, and to the work of the church. This legitimizes self expression and introspection and centers this responsibility within each individual; not one's spouse, nor a religious leader, but each member holds the key to self knowledge. There must also be a consequent need to let that personal awareness be expressed in daily life.

With the idea that "Actual grace is a now presence, a now sharing, a now gift," cursillistas address the immediacy of grace. Grace is not passé, but an ongoing phenomenon that is present in their everyday world. Actual grace is *au courant,* a happening, an event. The motto's impact rests on the usage of the "now" phrases at a time when they appear in common usage. The cursillo purposefully harnesses words that appeal, that are in vogue, and that are less taken for granted than others. In trying to avoid cliches, the cursillo uses current phrases to its advantage, getting its message across forcefully. Just as these terms strike a different chord in the individual's everyday world, they serve to impart cursillistas with a religious sense, as in the phrase "Jesus is where the action is." Individuals in our society generally equate "where the action is" with a place and setting where one ought to be; therefore this phrase shifts the direction from entertainment and vacation spots to religion and Christian community. The focal point for those who must be where the significant events occur is Jesus. He is the center of attraction, *the* person to be with, and the cursillistas begin to think about Jesus in terms generally used for celebrities and privileged individuals.

The parochial mottos emphasize the shift from a negative to a positive religious attitude that distinguishes the cursillo ideology. This is further seen in the line "If you live in fear of God, you may as well forget it." The traditional approach to God as Master, which encouraged the predominant feeling of fear, is negated; instead, the alternative is an accessible God who kindles hopeful feelings. This idea is reaffirmed in the motto "Talk to him as your brother" and in the line "It's a joy to be a true Christian." Many of the parochial mottos convey this spiritual orientation to religious life based on cheerfulness, sharing, and Christian love. They direct members to an intimate relationship with Christ, as well as encouraging warm and close bonds with other members. Yet whatever the specific meaning of each motto, it always echoes the regional spirit by being framed in existing idioms and current expressions.

To study both the generic and parochial mottos is to discover that many phrases pertain directly to traditional Catholic beliefs and practices. The phrase "A sad saint is a sorry saint" highlights the role of saints, a position found in the traditional church; it stresses the need for living a holy and sanctifying life. "Contact with Christ and with the brothers" acknowledges the significance of prayer, Mass, and Holy Communion—three major aspects of traditional Catholicism. Some of the generic mottos, such as "Sons of the Father, brother of Christ, temples of the Holy Spirit," are identical to traditional phrases. In this way, the mottos relate the cursillo doctrine to traditional Catholicism, reinforcing the unity between both, which aids to legitimate the movement.

But if mottos unite the cursillo with Catholicism, they simultaneously work to establish a distinctive difference between both. While referring to traditional practices, the mottos generally assert a position that deviates significantly from the traditional orientation. For example, "A sad saint is a sorry saint" does affirm the importance of sainthood, but that is not the complete message. It goes further to show that a sad saint, the general impression presented by traditional Catholicism concerning saints, is misdirected. This line denies the necessity of absolute suffering, or of a painful desolate existence, as a criterion of saintliness, implying instead a different stance based on a cheerful and optimistic attitude. It stresses salvation and sainthood through a hopeful existence, without the association of "sackcloth and ashes." For the cursillista, this motto also recalls the way of sainthood through the triple means of piety, study, and action, with the concomitant attitude of confidence and joy. Sadness is not a necessary factor in attaining saintliness, but a misconception perpetuated by traditional Catholicism. Moreover, holiness is not limited to a select few, but is a goal which all members should try to attain. Saintliness, unlike the traditional depiction, is not restricted to the few, the frail, and the suffering; in the cursillo it is a state which all Christians can attain. With the use of a few words, this motto recalls the importance of sainthood in Catholicism, presents the inadequate conception in the traditional approach, and implies the rectified cursillo position.

In a similar fashion "Contact with Christ and with the brothers" asserts the traditional significance of prayer and the need for communal participation at Mass and in the reception of Communion. Yet for the cursillista, this line implies forms of prayer that are not restricted to rote stanzas and standardized formulas. Contact with Christ, in the cursillo, embraces spontaneous prayer that encourages a continual response to daily events. It may be the dew on a hydrangea, the crimson of autumn leaves, or a smiling face—events that induce reflection from the cursillista. And this meditation, whether it be internally voiced or marked by the power of silence, is a prayer in its affirmation and celebration of life. Prayer is not only predictable and routinized; it is also open and spontaneous.

In addition, this "contact with Christ" is not a communication which requires intermediaries, such as angels and saints, but entails a direct interchange with Christ. Contact with Christ as one's brother, implies a close bond which undermines the role of traditional intermediaries. The need of brotherhood and sisterhood among cursillistas is also asserted, as is the importance of frequent gatherings, namely, the group reunions and the ultreyas. Christianity in the cursillo is an interpersonal experience, not the isolated individualized religion which frequently marks the traditional parish religion.

In this way, the generic and parochial mottos express and embody the relationship between the system of discontents and the system of beliefs in the cursillo. The mottos, while aligning themselves with Catholicism, simultaneously oppose certain aspects of the traditional approach and present the "corrected" cursillo position.

In conclusion, the cursillo movement can be explained as a reexamination of *Christianity*. Hervas and Bonnin and their followers continually confront Christianity, uncoiling the previous definitions which mark the past centuries of the church. The cursillo returns to the early definitions of Christianity, expressed in the New Testament and manifested in the lives of the first to call themselves Christians.

The cursillo began and continues to be a process of rethinking terms, ideas, and beliefs that are ritualisitically taken for granted in the church. Words such as *grace, sin, saintliness,* and *prayer* are seen as cliches in the traditional Catholic context, having lost their force to provoke reflection and spawn action. The cursillo excavates the language of Catholicism, hollowing out the antiquated images which no longer initiate action. In other words, the cursillo wrestles a new language from the old language of Catholicism, providing what it would consider a more exact Christianity.

The cursillo's distinguishing dimension and the mark of its creativity rests in its ability to "say again" with force, clarity and persuasion what has been both inferred and stated at some point in the past centuries of Catholic tradition. The focus of self, family, and environment, as well as the techniques of piety, study, and action are not new ideas. But the unexpected linking of these particular dimensions in triadic relationships is a creative endeavor, as are the associated images, metaphors, and conceptions aligned with them.

It is in the sense of image, metaphor, and analogy that the cursillo is a renewal movement. The cursillo uses Catholic rituals and beliefs, but not in the sense of replication, for the cursillo involves a "misuse" of Catholic tradition; ideas and images are purposefully altered. This continual "misdirection" is viewed as a *correction* of the previous Catholic tradition, the rectifying of inappropriate and lifeless images and ideas.

In a word, and returning again to Geertz, the cursillo is a *model of* and a *model for* Catholicism. Its program and method presents a better way to be Catholic; cursillistas adapt Christian doctrine to their particular social and historical situations. The alterations of the cursillo are not seen as a deviation from Catholicism, but as a more accurate expression of Catholicism.

The new images, analogies, and metaphors of the cursillo are a radical criticism of the tradition that precedes

The Language of a Movement

it. In fact, the cursillo not only implies this position, but also provides the basis for, and the continuation of, this criticism, by its very existence. It remains to be seen whether the cursillo can continue to renew its own language or whether the cursillo itself will need the impetus and creative step which another movement will provide. The question, perhaps, is not whether a radical criticism of the cursillo will take place, but when it will occur.

> When a writer is no longer capable of thus founding a new universality and of taking the risk of communicating, he has outlived his time. It seems to me that we can also say of institutions that they have ceased to live when they show themselves incapable of carrying on a poetry of human relations—that is, the call of each individual freedom to all the others.[9]

The cursillo has been willing to risk, because what it values is well expressed in "carrying on a poetry of human relations." It is not easy; poetry, as Hölderlin knew, is a most difficult and dangerous possession. But there is a realization in the cursillo that people can effect and maintain "a poetry of human relations." Yes, the cursillo is an attempt at poetry; it is itself a poem in action, and it is as difficult to understand and interpret as a major poetic text.

In this way we understand the cursillo as a hermeneutics of a text, the movement itself as poetry and the texts as efforts to convey and express the human dimension. Above all, it is the realization that "speech is the invocation of our own being in concert with others."[10] At Ocean Bay, the language of the cursillo seems to be the "invocation of . . . being" because it dramatically transforms the way of life of its members. Yet, in time, the language of the cursillo may become a mimicry of itself, falling into

Analysis of the Movement

the same pattern as the traditional structure that it has always criticized. Like the writer who has "outlived his time," the cursillo, when addressing its discontents with Catholicism, may fail to establish "a new universality" or may simply cease "the risk of communicating."

Since poetry is difficult to maintain, we sense its flow, its direction, and its end, knowing that there will come a time when the poetry cannot be sustained and others or another movement will continue the poetic rhythm; the unfolding poem will be different as it reaches beyond the cursillo to restate and to give witness to the dynamics of human relations and praxis.

Some individuals assume that this has already occurred. The very factors which the cursillo stresses, namely, emotional expression, critical reflection, study, and action, become the very reasons why individuals leave the cursillo and join other movements. Since members are encouraged to reflect, study, and take an active part in Christian life, they also at some time reflect not only on the Catholic church and its tradition, but also on the very movement that upholds this position. Whether the cursillo perceives itself as exempt from critical reflection or not, it becomes, at some point and for certain individuals, part of the process of a critical religious evaluation. When this occurs, there are times the cursillo is appraised as less than it ideally should be, as failing itself in some of its objectives. Although it asks individuals to reflect, the cursillo limits the dynamics of this contemplation by steering people to particular preselected books and periodicals. In specifying action and community interaction, the cursillo does not generate a role for expansive community involvement, restricting its response to many socially perceived needs and social reforms in American society. Because the cursillo is geared to religious action, more clearly defined as cursillo-related action, many members are caught in contradictions, left without any encouragement or plan of action for prison reform, drug rehabilitation, or affirmative action issues. In this sense, the cursillo could never provide the vehicle for the more active, liberal membership of the church; its notion of reform is focused within the church and, more specifically, towards middle-class individuals. Remembering that membership for the cursillo is generally limited to middle-class Catholics and that the movement avoids alcoholics, those with any previous mental problems, and those with drug dependencies, the cursillo eliminates from its memberships those that pose added difficulty. And these membership criteria reflect its ideological orientation and its middle-class prejudices. Also, using any standards of religious affirmative action, if there should be such a standard, the cursillo would be judged discriminatory in many respects. The fact that women cannot join until their husbands have first become members reflects a restricted image of women. It also serves to place many women at the whims of their husbands. Thus actions are not always consistent with the mottos, so that, "To attain an ideal, you've got to be you" becomes, for many women, appended to the idea, "given that it is acceptable to your husband."

Thus what occurs is that such ideals as "Contact with Christ and with the brothers" can be narrowly interpreted, which some members judge unChristian. For "the brothers" does not include all individuals, but generally just middle-class Catholics. Given no satisfactory role for liberal social reform, many discover in the cursillo the way to open a door which leads beyond the confines of the movement.

In addition, the emphasis on joy and peace may become programmed, with witnessing necessarily being happy and exuberant. For some, freedom is stifled in the rigidity of the Leaders' School. Organized and programmed, some discern a lack of the spontaneity they had come to expect and demand of the movement. Certain members also begin to value the emotional expression encouraged in the cursillo, seeking out more occasions and rituals marked by self expression and spontaneity. Yet the cursillo endorses only a moderate degree of emotional response, upholding the middle-class norms for what is deemed appropriate behavior. Those wanting more than the de colores embrace and witnessing find there is no space for this self expression in the cursillo. Thus, some go in search of more.

Through the cursillo, individuals are reacquainted with earlier Christianity, with its emphasis on a dynamic apostolate and on becoming disciples of Christ. The stress on earlier Christianity, the sense of Pentecost, and an active faith leads some members to want more than the cursillo provides. Some seek out the other aspects of the earlier church, as they turn to charismatic groups and prayer healing.

Others, reestablished as a couple through the cursillo and identifying more with being married than they previously did, share with their spouses in study, action, and piety; they find they want more of a sense of coupleness than could be expected to characterize a movement based on the linking of individual Christians in a Christian community. Initiations, the work of team leaders, and many of the group reunions are segregated by sex so that couples are inevitably split, not united, in some of the cursillo activities. Wanting another direction, some take leave of the cursillo for an active role in marriage encoun-

The Language of a Movement

ters where the focus is specifically directed to the married couple.

So the cursillo entered as a force within the church, and we can predict without clairvoyance that it will at some point disappear. To follow four lines from a poem:

> Page after page, the old man goes on with it,
> Making way for the everlasting
> Next, which exerts its power
> By withholding its presence.[11]

The cursillo attempts with all its structure, orientation, rite of passage, and doctrinal elaborations to make present that which has not been clearly evident within the church. In some way, the cursillo succeeds when meaningfulness, exhilaration, and awareness seize a member's life; and views shift and become more significant. Yet "that which withdraws," as Heidegger also was aware, does not itself disappear, even when there is some presencing. So the withdrawal continues, and that which has "presenced" itself begins to join the arena of the withdrawal until the cursillo's success must be reckoned also as a failure.

Yet to say that the cursillo fails is not to say that it has no impact. It is rather to appreciate the cursillo as a human enterprise which must fail since all human attempts are incomplete, impermanent, and in flux. Hervas, Bonnin, and all others significantly involved in the leadership of the movement could say, if they so recognized it, the words of e. e. cummings, "An artist, a man, a failure, *must proceed.*"[12] And the procession may be the very transformation of the cursillo into a form that is quite distinct from itself, yet developed from its very core. Perhaps unrecognizable in the metamorphosis of these future forms, these developments from the cursillo will

Analysis of the Movement

follow. Already, charismatics, social activists, marriage encounters, and prayer healing are cases in point.

Returning to the poem, we find again it speaks to the cursillo:

> the names
> he listens for are the ones
> omitted, rejected, unnamed. The old man
>
> returns (a passion imitating an action)
> to failure, to the new occasion
> for failure, faithful to failure.[13]

The cursillo listened, seeking out the "omitted" in joyfulness, in Christian love, in action, as it sought out the "unnamed" in de colores, palancas, rollos, and as it rejected bureaucratization and secular values. But the omitted, the rejected, and the unnamed will always remain, not grasped despite all the efforts of the cursillo, and thus in its success is also its disappointment. For what is victory but the failure of that which must, of necessity, withdraw. Out of each occasion to say is an occasion not to say, and with each naming there still remains, to use one of Ruth Benedict's phrases, "the brief flowers of no name." So that the cursillo, like all movements, is not only a new way to see and experience the world but is also a precursor of other movements. Just as language is never complete or finished, but in process, so too is the cursillo, even when its momentum no longer resembles itself.

This also means that the cursillo may also lose sight of its own message, that the memory of its past and its first clear perspective of the Catholic church may blind it to a critique of itself. So intent on assessing the problems of Catholicism, the cursillo may forget that now it has become part of the very process it once attacked and may fail to throw critical glances in its own direction. This

The Language of a Movement

does not mean that others, however, outside the cursillo, and less emotionally attached to its structure, will not critically examine it, pointing out the areas of the forgotten and the omitted. Because our tendency is not to remember but to forget, we can expect the cursillo to forget its attack against secularism, bureaucracy, and its own message of change and revitalization, so that it exists without directing critical thoughts to its own structure. Remaining static, it will then fall in to the very religious trap it once held against traditional Catholicism.

Whether the cursillo will be a passing movement, an opened door to another pathway, or whether this movement will become a stronger, more vibrant force in the revitalization of Christianity remains to be seen. Its direction and journey lies ahead, forged in the very historical choices taken. Yet what we do know and must remember is that the ontological dimension involves a continual search, that is both the cursillo's raison d'être and means of expansion as well as its potential failure and transformation. Today the cursillo veers inevitably toward this crossroad. Only the steps taken will provide the direction. For this answer, all of us—members, social scientists, and readers must wait.

Notes

1. M. Heidegger in W. Biemel, "Poetry and Language in Heidegger," in *On Heidegger and Language,* ed. J. Kockelmans (Evanston: Northwestern University Press, 1972), p. 80.

2. M. Heidegger, *Poetry, Language, Thought,* trans. A. Hofstadter (New York, Harper and Row, 1975).

3. J. Derrida, *Speech and Phenomena,* trans. D. Allison, (Evanston: Northwestern University Press, 1973), p. 104.

4. Ibid., p. 102.

5. Ibid., p. 107.

6. Ibid., p. 108.

7. J. Hervas, *Cursillos in Christianity—Instrument of Christian Renewal,* trans. W. Young (Phoenix: Ultreya Press, 1965), p. 265.

8. T. S. Eliot, *Four Quartets* (New York: Harcourt, Brace and World, Inc., 1943), p. 19.

9. M. Merleau-Ponty, *The Prose of the World,* trans. J. O'Neill (Evanston: Northwestern University Press, 1973), p. xiii.

10. J. O'Neill, Translator's Introduction, "Language and the Voice of Philosophy," Ibid., p. xxx.

11. R. Howard, "Prose for Borges," in *Prose for Borges,* ed. C. Newman and M. Kinzie (Evanston: Northwestern University Press, 1972), p. 3.

12. e. e. cummings, *Six Non-Lectures* (New York: Atheneum Press, 1968), p. 80.

APPENDIX

METHODS AND ASSUMPTIONS: TURNING THE PERISCOPE INWARD

In research, one never totally succeeds, for one ultimately falls short of certain objectives, particularly if one's goal is not just explanation but understanding. One never fully comprehends social phenomena. Instead, there is a grasp of correlations, the formulation of various premises, and the analysis of data. In other words, the researcher arrives at a *perspective* on social phenomenon. The value of this perspective lies in its consistency, its insights, and its heuristic potential. This judgment, however, is never the privilege of the researcher, but belongs to his and her scientific audience. Since the writer is "someone to whom the *last word* is denied; to write is to offer others, from the start, that last word."[1]

Yet before the last word is given, a few more words need to be said. In one sense, this research is a study of one religious movement, the leaders who established it, and those who follow their teachings. To this extent, it is a monograph of the cursillo, illustrating the history, beliefs, and methods of the movement. A motivation for selecting the cursillo rests in the fact that no research has been undertaken by anthropologists on this religious movement. Not only have anthropologists avoided the cursillo, but also they have generally disregarded examining Roman Catholicism. In addition, I purposefully sought to research a movement within the United States. As mentioned earlier, too frequently anthropologists present non-Western movements as strange and exotic phenomena, and they generally overlook the curious and extraordinary behavior occurring within the confines of their own culture. Thus I chose to seek out the unusual within American culture and specifically among middle-class individuals.

Participant observation was a significant technique in understanding the cursillo, since it provides a quality of

Appendix

data derived from continuous face-to-face interactions. It is the technique that most clearly symbolizes the social sciences, with its rigorous analysis, its continual examination of behavior, yet its flexibility and its concern for the innuendos of everyday life, or as Malinowski terms this aspect, the "imponderabilia of actual life." For he, more than other anthropologists at his time, realized that:

> There is a series of phenomena of great importance which cannot possibly be recorded by questioning or computing documents, but have to be observed in their full actuality.[2]

The two following research situations based on participant observations were critical in accumulating data on the cursillo:

Informal Meetings and Visits

These were casual meetings with members of the cursillo and with noninitiated individuals. First, there were the unexpected meetings where I encountered an individual shopping, walking, or relaxing on a park bench. Depending on the situation, we would talk over coffee or, standing where we met, discuss cursillo-related events. At such times, I was informed about forthcoming meetings, new sponsorships or other specifics on the cursillo.

A second type of informal discussion occurred when I or a cursillista would "stop in" for a morning coffee break, or for a glass of wine after supper. These get-togethers were generally an hour or two hours long, with a variety of topics discussed. During the initial stage of research, these meetings entailed less cursillo material as personal, family, and community issues dominated the discussions. These visits were of prime importance because I acquired informants and established myself as one "interested" in the cursillo.

Attendance at Regularly Scheduled Meetings

I was not initiated into the cursillo because of personal, and I might add, ethical reasons. Members frequently asked if they could sponsor me, yet I continually refused their offer. Since I met all the requirements for initiation, individuals were anxious to have me partake in the experience. Many assumed that I was interested in joining the cursillo and gathered that in time I would be converted. Some even mentioned that the power of the cursillo message could be judged, in the end, by whether I would eventually submit to initiation and thereby to living the cursillo.

Through my informants, I was allowed to attend the group meetings, the ultreyas, and organizational meetings of the secretariat. When greeted with de colores, I returned the embrace with a thank-you instead of echoing the cursillo phrase, signaling to the particular individuals that I was not a cursillista. There was never any pretense of my being initiated, which became advantageous, since I was excused from responding to such questions as "What apostolic success did the Lord accomplish through you this week?" and "What was the moment in which you felt closest to Christ?" I could sit, listen, and observe, being freed from responding to the many inquiries. At these meetings I acquired data on the doctrine and the method of the cursillo as it was translated in the everyday life of its members. It was here that I came to under-

Appendix

stand the regional transformation of the structure Hervas founded.

To claim I relied on participant observation is not to say my research was limited to participation and observation. As McCall and Simmons well know:

> participant observation is not a single method but rather a characteristic style of research which makes use of a number of methods and techniques—observation, informant interviewing, document analysis, respondent interviewing, and participation with self-analysis.[3]

Particpant observation entails certain methodological assumptions regardless of the variety of techniques employed. One such assumption is that there are reciprocal influences of researchers and their subjects where, as Maurice Stein so clearly understands, social scientists are "participating victims" in addition to particpating observers of the "forces" they investigate.[4] The following two research situations allude to this orientation.

Informal Interviews

These meetings were initiated primarily for acquiring data on the cursillo. Even though research was the raison d'être of these gatherings, they were informal because the situations were also intended as social events. For example, members who knew of my interest in the cursillo would extend invitations for dinner. Frequently, we ate a late meal, lingering over supper with little disclosed about the cursillo until the dinner dishes were cleared and everyone relaxed. I could never predict how much time would be devoted to cursillo issues, for it varied from one family to another, and from one occasion to another. If there were young children, the discussions on the cursillo would not occur until they were asleep; the time of this varies among households. Also, if the husband or wife had an unusually trying day, the conversations remained peripheral to cursillo issues. To be sure, these social situations did not lend themselves to note taking, so I relied on several mnemonic devices which provided keys in reconstructing the discussions.

At times, these informal interviews occurred in restaurants. In this context, I found it more difficult for members to concentrate on the specifics of the movement. The clashing of dishes, the waiters' interruptions, the sounds of nearby conversations and programmed music were just a few of the many, constant distractions. As a result, individuals were less apt to speak continuously about the cursillo in restaurants than in their homes. Moreover, I found it more difficult to remember key words in this situation; when interviewing at someone's home, I could write down information in my car immediately after leaving. When the interviews took place in restaurants, I was sometimes driven home, with more time elapsing before I could record major points.

Formal Interviews: Focused and Non-Focused

In the formal interviews, the social interaction was designed specifically for acquiring data. In the beginning stages of research, I used the tape recorder whenever it did not inhibit the exchange of information. In the early seventies, it was not unusual for a member to refuse an interview if I insisted on using the recorder. The secrecy

Appendix

code at that time instilled discomfort about disclosure that was heightened with the presence of the recorder. Some cursillistas hinted that the tapes could be used against them as a testimony of their unfaithfulness to the secrecy code. Therefore, I asked members if they objected to being taped, and whenever they indicated a preference for note taking, I resorted to this approach. Unexpectedly, the most informative and spirited interviews occurred without the tape recorder; individuals conversed for hours, undisturbed by the tape recording. Some of the taped interviews did reveal pertinent doctrinal and personal information, but generally not to the extent or intensity of those interviews occurring without the microphone and tapes. As I became more comfortable with the interview situation, increasingly anticipating the unexpectedness of these unusual interactions—the discussion, disclosure, and the "telling of their story"—I abandoned the tape recorder and discovered the substitute of pen and paper more exciting and freeing. The absence of the tape recorder opened the possibility for greater disclosure and far more rewarding interactions. It is clear that there is a style of interviewing that is more amenable to personal recording of information, where the flow of words to paper is not static and artificial, as can occur with the recorder, but in contrast, more genuine, trustful, and revealing of people's feelings and thoughts.

Most of the formal interviews took place in private homes. Generally I traveled to the member's home, although in some cases the person opted to meet at mine. Some interviews involved questioning both marriage partners during the same situation, but the majority entailed only one individual being interviewed. Meetings with two individuals at the same time were problematic; husbands, for example, answered for their wives, or both spoke simultaneously. Where possible, I established separate interviews, yet whenever a couple insisted on being questioned together I assented.

Analysis of Documents

Unlike many anthropologists who study nonliterate groups, I was researching an articulate and literate social group, allowing the analysis of documents. The cursillo's focus on study and the emphasis on uniformity of doctrine encourages the proliferation of documents. In the beginning stages of research, however, I was unaware of these documents that certainly would have afforded insight into the cursillo program. Early access to these documents would have elicited more pertinent information, thereby establishing, from an earlier time, the dynamics of the cursillo framework. More important, I would have received more data from informants at Ocean Bay during this stage of research because my fluency in cursillo terminology would have allayed their fear of disclosure.

Without texts, without many informants, I was initially lost in the sphere of a new language, without "dictionary" and without "grammer." I was not mute, however, and continued raising question after question. The first months were extremely confusing and frustrating; the secrecy code remained quite problematic. Members enjoyed discussing issues about the church, parish activities, Vatican II, but when I returned to the topic of the cursillo, there was evasion and silence. For a period I was stymied.

Gradually, however, a few individuals consented to discuss the cursillo openly, launching a breakthrough. As I acquired a familiarity with such terms as palanca, de colores, decuria, rollo, and others, cursillistas assumed I

Appendix

knew the entire structure and began discussing any issue without reservation. From this point on, gathering data was expedited, with my information increasing geometrically. The members began disclosing certain documents, providing an overwhelming amount of resources on the cursillo. Within a few more months, I possessed all the material given to members of the Leaders' School.

The following list comprises the documents which were significant in analyzing the cursillo:

Major Texts

Alcuin, W.; Barry, L.; et al. *Spiritual Director's Manual.* Dallas: A National Ultreya Publication, 1976.

Bonnin, E., et al. *Structure of Ideas.* Phoenix: Ultreya Press, 1965.

Capo, J. *Lower Your Nets.* Phoenix: Ultreya Press, 1969.

──── *The Group Reunion: Theory and Practice.* Phoenix: Ultreya Press, 1969.

Clark, S. and Martin, R. *The Purpose of the Movement.* Dallas: A National Ultreya Publication, 1974.

Hervas, J. *Cursillos in Christianity: Instrument of Christian Renewal.* Phoenix: Ultreya Press, 1965.

──── *Leaders' Manual for Cursillos in Christianity.* Phoenix: Ultreya Press, 1964.

──── *Questions and Problems.* Phoenix: Ultreya Press, 1966.

Cursillo

National Secretariat. *The Three Days*. Dallas: A National Ultreya Publication, 1972.

National Secretariat of Venezuela, Coordinator. *The Fundamental Ideas of the Cursillo Movement*. Dallas: A National Ultreya Publication, 1974.

Rohloff, I. *The Origins and Development of Cursillo*. Dallas: A National Ultreya Publication, 1976.

Major Pamphlets

Blatnik, A. *Your Fourth Day*. Dallas: A National Ultreya Publication.

Bonnin, E. et al. *The Cursillo Movement: The Cursillo Weekend*. Dallas: A National Ultreya Publication.

⸻. *The Cursillo Movement: Explanation and Purpose*. Dallas: A National Ultreya Publication.

⸻. *The Cursillo Movement: The Essential Principles*. Dallas: A National Ultreya Publication.

⸻. *The Cursillo Movement: The Precursillo*. Dallas: A National Ultreya Publication.

⸻. *The How and the Why*. Phoenix: Ultreya Press, 1966.

Capo, J. *The Cursillo, Yesterday and Today*. Dallas: A National Ultreya Publication.

Clark, S. *The Work of the Cursillos and the Work of Renewal*. Phoenix: Ultreya Press, 1967.

Appendix

Duran, A. *The Essence and Purpose.* Phoenix: Ultreya Press, 1962.

⸺ *The Cursillos in Christianity Movement.* Phoenix: Ultreya Press, 1966.

Hughes, G., Coordinator. *Leaders' School: Statements from Various Cursillo Sources.* Dallas: A National Ultreya Publication.

Mulligan, F. *The Reunion of the Group.* Phoenix: Ultreya Press, 1967.

Platt, G. *The Cursillos in Christianity Movement.* Phoenix: Ultreya Press, 1962.

Taylor, D. *The Pastor and the Cursillo Movement.* Kalamazoo: Kalamazoo Publishing Company, 1966.

Mimeographed Articles

Bonnin, E. "The Essential, the Important and the Accidental Elements in the Cursillo."

⸺ "Procedure of the Group Meeting."

Clark, S. and Martin, R. "Cursillo Talks—An Overview."

Clore, V. "That the World May Know . . . "

Conlan, T. "What Happened to the Cursillo . . . ?"

"Ecumenical Endeavors."

"Giving a Rollo at the Ultreya."

Higgins, J. "Mortification."

Izquierdo, P. "The Psychology of the Newly Converted in the Cursillo."

Montero, C. "Speaking of the National Ultreya."

Moran, T. "Involvement of a Weekend."

"The Call to be a Rollista."

"The Cursillo Leader."

"The Cursillo Movement."

"The Group Reunion."

"The Purpose of the Ultreya."

"Ultreya: Weekly Reunion."

Mimeographed Material: Organizational Data

"Criteria for Selection of Rectors and Rectoras."

"Explanation of Group Reunion."

"History of Activities Related to Post-Cursillo."

"Leaders' School General Norms."

"Post-Cursillo Resource Committee."

"Pre-Cursillo Guidelines."

"Preparing a Rollo."

"Proposed Outline for Introduction to Cursillo."

"Purpose of the Diocesan Secretariat."

"Quick Refresher on Highlights on Group Reunion Format."

"Role of Committee Leaders at the Ultreya."

"Selection of Cursillo Candidates."

"Sponsor Requirements."

Appendix

"Study of Environments."

"Ultreya."

"Ultreya Committee By-Laws."

Mimeographed Material Given to the Initiate

"Conclusion—A Summary of Rollo Titles: An Ideal."

"Cursillo Application Form."

"De Colores Song Sheet."

"Meditation."

"Palanca."

"Proposed Questionnaire for Persons Who Have Attended the Cursillo."

"Putting It All Together."

"Service Sheet."

"Spanish Phrases Used during the Cursillo."

Reports of National Cursillo Meetings

Annual Report of the Executive Director.

First Latin-American Encounter of National Delegates of the Cursillos in Christianity. Bogota, August 14–17, 1968.

First National Encounter of Cursillo Leaders in the United States of America. South Bend, Indiana, July 28–30, 1971.

Proceedings of the Sixth National Conference. Lansing, Michigan, 1965.

Cursillo

Second World Encounter of National Delegates of the Cursillos in Christianity. Tlazcala, Mexico, May 17–21, 1970.

The Third Session of Leaders National Sharing Workshop. Madrid, Spain, February, 1968.

Journal Articles on the Cursillo

Hervas, J. "The 'Cursillos de Cristiandad': (Part I)." *Christ to the World.* No. 2, 1962.

———. "The 'Cursillos de Cristiandad': (Part II)." *Christ to the World.* No. 2, 1962.

Jacobs, W. "The Cursillo: What is It and Does It Work?" *Ave Maria.* January 22, 1964.

Maldonato, M. "I Went to a Cursillo: Testimony of a Layman." *Christ to the World.* No. 6, 1964.

Petru, A. "The Cursillos de Cristiandad: Their Structure." *Christ to the World.* No. 6, 1964.

Cursillo Newsletter and Magazine

The Cursillo Movement: Newsletter of the National Secretariat of the Cursillo Movement in the United States.

Ultreya Magazine (National Magazine of the Cursillos in Christianity).

Personal Documents

Diaries written during initiation.

Rollos presented at various initiations.

Palancas received as initiates.

Palancas presented to other initiates.

Appendix

Not only did these documents provide information on the basic framework of the cursillo, but they were necessary in evaluating the degree of doctrinal and methodological consistency of the group at Ocean Bay when compared to the general designs of Hervas and Bonnin. While some documents illustrated a close allegiance to the ideals and directives of Hervas, others demonstrated the particular regional tone expressed at Ocean Bay. In particular, the diaries and texts of rollos were invaluable personal testimony to the variations and deviations within the cursillo groups.

My research on the cursillo involved the strict, rigorous use of the previously discussed techniques. These are the scientific tools which afforded the data and the insight to accomplish a study of the cursillo de cristiandad. Yet I must add that, in another sense, this research is not only a study of this religious movement but also a study of social change. It provides a definite, although rudimentary, theoretical framework for examining religious innovation. The cursillista's phrase that "The cursillo begins when it ends" well applies to this research, for further study and reflection on change, creativity, and metaphorical innovation begins when the research of this religious movement ends. Some of the premises related to this aspect of religious social innovation are:

1. Creativity stems from a "mistranslation" or a "misinterpretation" of a past traditional position.

2. Doubts as well as beliefs shape the new ideology since both are necessary in the process of mistranslation.

3. Legitimation of the new system entails a neces-

sary reliance on tradition with a "misuse" of this tradition to the advantage of the new system.

4. The "success" of the new system requires the receptivity of an audience to both doubts and beliefs.

5. Charisma, when present, does not displace tradition, but is interwoven with this source of authority.

My understanding of the cursillo is derived from two sources, namely: (1) the ongoing social phenomenon and (2) my conceptual and perceptual framework. I cannot conclude this chapter without discussing the influence of the latter on my interpretation of the cursillo. No one perceives social phenomenon without certain assumptions which affect, to some extent and degree, his or her understanding. For this reason, it behooves all researchers to make these premises clear. Yet the task is a difficult one, not only because it is a self-stripping process to reveal one's personal premises, but because they are not generally self-evident. They remain hidden and do not easily surface. Some premises never surface due to repression, fear, and ignorance. So one has to dig, dissect, and probe. This process of radical reflection is not easily accomplished, but demands rigorous thinking and systematic introspection.

My work involves many premises about social behavior which have guided both the techniques and the interpretation of data. Some of these dominant assumptions are:

1. An investigation of social phenomenon is simultaneously an investigation of the social scientist and her discipline, linking all research with metascientific concerns.

Appendix

2. The most significant, yet most difficult process, resulting in insight and understanding, stems from confronting the dimensions of social life that are taken for granted.

3. The social, historical, and cultural context of the investigating researcher critically shapes her data.

4. Analysis of social phenomenon entails the grasping of the previous historical form, as well as the present structural framework, in order to uncover the dynamic transformative processes.

5. Understanding is derived from a confrontation with social phenomenon that is ultimately strange, puzzling, and mysterious.

6. The shocks of fieldwork are as much the result of one's class as the result of one's culture.

7. The confrontation of paradox is significant in uncovering new cognitive modalities, in the clarification of scientific concepts, and in the discovery of knowledge.

To say my research is influenced by these premises does not imply that I was unaffected by the social behavior I investigated. I was. My presentation of the cursillo is not an artistic reaction, nor a novel, but a work of scientific research. By scientific, I infer a direct relationship between my personal, professional conceptualization and the ongoing social behavior of cursillistas. To this extent, this research is not "what is it like to be a cursillista" but a presentation of one perspective among many possible ones. Through the particular orientation shaped by the social, historical, and cultural situation in which I exist, I offer an interpretation of the cursillo.

This does not mean my work is false. One should not confuse a perspective-based approach with one that is fictitious. To indicate that research is based on one's perspective is to stress that I perceive and conceptualize through a socially constructed system which affects, to some degree, my delineation of social reality. To me this epistemological stand is enlightening, but to one who maintains that the social sciences are absolute and strictly objective, this orientation may appear threatening.

If my presentation on the cursillo is only one among many perspectives, what criteria can be used to distinguish and evaluate the worth of this version? There are many factors, but the following are probably the most signficant:

1. The training and secondary socialization of the researcher, namely, academic graduate and postgraduate program.
2. Legitimation of the researcher's position within the specialized discipline.
3. The internal consistency of the presentation.
4. An illuminating and insightful presentation which clarifies social behavior.

There is, of course, a fifth criterion, and this is the restudy of the phenomenon by other social scientists and the comparative analysis of the various perspectives. Surely a restudy is a worthwhile outcome of any research. Nevertheless, restudies are not frequently undertaken in anthropology, except for a few classic cases as the Oscar Lewis–Robert Redfield studies of Tepoztlan.[5] It appears as if a restudy is threatening to anthropologists, especially to those who assume that objectivity and truth are attainable objectives. Here, a restudy of their work is judged

Appendix

not only as unnecessary for the properly trained researcher, but, moreover, it is viewed as the mark of failure in their scientific venture. I suggest, however, that a restudy is the mark of successful research, generating enthusiasm and interest in other researchers and leading them to confront the same social phenomenon. It is the sign of a successful teacher (or prophet), who can initiate action and motivate others to follow in her footsteps.

By holding the assumption that social phenomenon is illuminated, not destroyed, by various interpretations, the researcher is not threatened by different interpretations of her data and her subject, but encourages this. As Jacques Maquet well understands:

> Several perspectivistic views of the same social phenomenon help to describe more precisely each viewpoint and consequently to determine how each of them affects the resulting knowledge. . . . More is to be expected from the confrontation of a multiplicity of perspectives than from the quest for the "best one."[6]

Other perspectives are not competitors in the search for truth, but part of the process of understanding social phenomenon that is always and inevitably complex and ever changing.

To be sure, some will ask what type of epistemological stance such an orientation generates, or if truth is disregarded. Without a doubt, epistemology continues to be crucial in this approach; however, it will differ from the traditional epistemological concerns of the field. In the past, anthropologists have been extremely concerned with the issue of objectivity, based on the separation of object and subject. This notion of objectivity is one of the many traditional orientations derived from the natural sciences, from which anthropology borrowed many techniques, standards of research, and attitudinal orientations.[7] To a new science in its embryonic stage, this reliance on the natural sciences afforded security and legitimation. However, this borrowing impeded anthropology because the goals, standards, and directives were unclear and, at times, nonapplicable.

Caught in this web of natural science borrowing is the problem of objectivity. Standards are generally established in anthropology emphasizing the acquisition of data and its interpretation as distinct from the researcher's frame of reference. This rule is affirmed in the often-quoted phrase of a "value-free social science." As an orientation, it is exemplified in Pelto's *Anthropological Research* where he states that:

> anthropologists need to develop research methods that protect the researcher from his own subjective assumptions and value judgments.[8]

Here is a case where the anthropologist assumes that researchers can be protected from subjective influences and, implicitly, that such a cleavage of object and subject can resolve the problem of objectivity. However the traditional assumptions of objectivity, founded on the separation of subject and object, are misdirected. One cannot teach anthropologists to be objective although one can continue to voice the belief in objectivity, which is quite distinct from the former.

It is my position, based on training and research of the cursillo, that anthropology needs a *concretized epistemology,* one which searches for knowledge not in the abstract, but within concrete historical situations. What I suggest is an epistemology cognizant of the historical and social situation of the researcher, as well as the subjects of

Appendix

study. It is, in one sense, a personalized and humanistic epistemology. Yet such a position appears to involve a logical contradiction, that history and autobiography negate truth and knowledge. Without a doubt, the conretizing of epistemology is paradoxical, but it does not signal the end of epistemology, nor the denial of history or the personal dimension. Instead, it heralds the discovery of a different foundation of knowledge and the creation of new modalities of thought. I am quite certain that this is one of the most significant paradoxes facing present-day anthropology. Yet this new epistemology will only surface when the paradox is truly confronted by questioning and imaginative social scientists. In many ways it is to come face-to-face with Heidegger's intriguing assumption that what is "most thought-provoking in our thought-provoking time is that we are still not thinking."[9]

With this, I end my words, allowing others the final word on this research—my readers, my colleagues, my friends. In one sense, however, I cannot bring this study of the cursillo to its proper conclusion, as if anthropologists ever fully complete their investigation of social phenomenon. And thus I echo the words of Paul Valéry: "One does not finish a work, one abandons it."

Cursillo

Notes

1. R. Barthes, *Critical Essays* (Evanston: Northwestern University Press, 1972), p. xi.

2. B. Malinowski, *Argonauts of the Western Pacific* (New York: E. P. Dutton and Company, 1961), p. 18.

3. G. McCall and J. Simmons, *Issues in Participant Observation* (Reading: Addison-Wesley, 1969), p. i.

4. Maurice Stein, *The Eclipse of Community* (New York: Harper and Row, 1964).

5. O. Lewis, *Life in a Mexican Village: Tepoztlan Restudied* (Urbana: University of Illinois Press, 1960). R. Redfield, *Tepoztlan—A Mexican Village* (Chicago: University of Chicago Press, 1930).

6. J. Maquet, "Objectivity in Anthropology" in *Current Anthropology* (Vol. 5, 1964), p. 54.

7. A. Kaplan, *The Conduct of Inquiry: Methodology for Behavioral Science* (San Francisco: Chandler Publishing Company, 1964).

8. P. Pelto, *Anthropological Research: The Structure of Inquiry* (New York: Harper and Row, 1970), p. 44.

9. M. Heidegger, *What is Called Thinking?*, trans. G. Gray (New York: Harper and Row, 1972), p. 6.

BIBLIOGRAPHY

Albert, E. "The Classification of Values: A Method and Illustration." *American Anthropologist* 58 (1956).

Anderson, E. *Messianic Popular Movements in the Lower Congo.* London: Kegan Paul, 1958.

Baeta, C. *Prophetism in Ghana: A Study of Some "Spiritual Churches."* London: Student Christian Movement Press, 1962.

Banton, M., ed. *Anthropological Approaches to the Study of Religion.* London: Tavistock, 1966.

Barber, B. "Acculturation and Messianic Movements." *American Sociological Review* 6 (1941).

Barrett, D. *Schism and Renewal in Africa.* London: Oxford University Press, 1968.

Barthes, R. *Critical Essays.* Evanston: Northwestern University Press, 1972.

Benedict, R. "Anthropology and the Humanities." *American Anthropologist* L, no. 4 (1948).

———. "Selected Poems." *An Anthropologist At Work: Writings of Ruth Benedict.* Edited by M. Mead. New York: Avon Books, 1973.

Bennetta, J. "The Veil of Objectivity: Prophecy, Divination and Social Inquiry." *American Anthropologist* (September 1978).

Berger, P. *The Sacred Canopy: Elements of a Sociological Theory of Religion.* New York: Doubleday and Company, 1969.

———, and Luckman, T. *The Social Construction of Reality.* New York: Doubleday and Company, 1967.

Bertsche, J. "Kimbanguism: A Separatist Movement." Master's thesis (Anthropology), Northwestern University, 1963.

Bibliography

Biemel, Walter. "Poetry and Language in Heidegger." In *On Heidegger and Language*. Edited by J. Kockelmans. Evanston: Northwestern University Press, 1972.

Bonnin, E. "The Essential, the Important, and the Accidental in the Cursillo Movement." Mimeographed, 1968.

――――. *The How and the Why*. Phoenix: Ultreya Press, 1966.

――――. "The Third Session of Leaders National Sharing Workshop." Mimeographed, 1968.

Bonnin, E.; Vadell, B.; and Forteza, Fr. *Structure of Ideas*. Phoenix: Ultreya Press, 1965.

Burke, K. *The Rhetoric of Religion: Studies in Logology*. Berkeley: University of California Press, 1970.

Burridge, K. "Cargo Cult Activity in Tangu." *Oceania* 24 (1954).

――――. *Mambu: A Study of Melanisian Cargo Movements and their Social and Ideological Background*. New York: Harper and Row, 1970.

Capo, J. *The Group Reunion*. Phoenix: Ultreya Press, 1969.

――――. *Lower Your Nets*. Phoenix: Ultreya Press, 1969.

Castaneda, C. *The Teachings of Don Juan: A Yaqui Way of Knowledge*. New York: Ballantine Books, 1969.

Clark, S. *The Work of the Cursillos and the Work of Renewal*. Phoenix: Ultreya Press, 1967.

Clark, S. and R. Martin. "Cursillo Talks—An Overview." Mimeographed, 1967.

———. *The Purpose of the Movement.* Dallas: A National Ultreya Publication, 1974.

Cohn, N. "Medieval Millenarism: Its Bearing on the Comparative Study of Millenarian Movements." In *Millenial Dreams in Action.* Edited by S. Thrupp. The Hague: Mouton and Company, 1962.

———. *The Pursuit of the Millenium.* London: Secken and Warburg, 1957.

cummings, e. e. *Six Non-Lectures.* New York: Atheneum Press, 1968.

Derrida, J. *Speech and Phenomena.* Translated by D. Allison. Evanston: Northwestern University Press, 1973.

Durkheim, E. *The Elementary Forms of Religious Life.* Glencoe: The Free Press, 1954.

Eliot, T. S. *Four Quartets.* New York: Harcourt, Brace and World, Inc., 1943.

Evans-Pritchard, E. *Nuer Religion.* Oxford: Clarendon Press, 1956.

———. *Primitive Theories of Religion.* Oxford: Clarendon Press, 1965.

Fabian, J. *Jamaa: A Charismatic Movement in Katanga.* Evanston: Northwestern University Press, 1971.

———. "Religion and Change." In *The African Experience.* Edited by J. Paden and E. Soja. Evanston: Northwestern University Press, 1970.

Fernandez, J. "African Religious Movements." *Journal of Modern African Studies* 2 (1964).

Firth, R. "Problem and Assumption in an Anthropological Study of Religion." *Journal of the Royal Anthropological Institute* 89 (1959).

Bibliography

———. *Tikopia Ritual and Belief.* London: George Allen Limited, 1967.

Friedrich, C. "For a Sociological Concept of Charisma." *Social Forces* 63 (1964).

Geertz, C. "Ideology as a Cultural System." In *Ideology and its Discontent.* Edited by D. Apter. New York: The Free Press, 1964.

———. "Religion as a Cultural System." In *Anthropological Approaches to the Study of Religion.* Edited by M. Banton. New York: F. A. Praeger, 1966.

Goody, J. "Religion and Ritual: The Definitional Problem." *British Journal of Sociology* 12 (1961).

Guiart, J. "Culture Contact and the 'John Frum' Movements on Tanna, New Hebrides." *Southwest Journal of Anthropology* 12 (1956).

Harris, M. *Cows, Pigs, Wars and Witches: The Riddles of Culture.* New York: Vintage Books, 1974.

Hegel, G. *Early Theological Writings.* Translated by T. Knox. Chicago: The University of Chicago Press, 1948.

———. *On Art, Religion, Philosophy.* Edited by J. Glenn. New York: Harper Torchbook, 1970.

Heidegger, M. "Hölderlin and the Essence of Poetry." In *European Literary Theory and Practice: From Existential Phenomenology to Structuralism.* Edited by V. Gras. New York: Delta Books, 1973.

———. *Poetry, Language, Thought.* Translated by A. Hofstadter. New York: Harper and Row, 1975.

———. *What is Called Thinking?* Translated by G. Gray. New York: Harper and Row, 1972.

Hervas, J. "The 'Cursillos de Cristiandad' (Part I)." *Christ to the World* 2 (1962).

———. "The 'Cursillos de Chrsitiandad' (Part II)." *Christ to the World* 2 (1962).

———. *Cursillos in Christianity—Instrument of Christian Renewal.* Translated by W. Young. Phoenix: Ultreya Press, 1965.

———. *Leaders' Manual for Cursillos in Christianity.* Translated by C. Portnoff and M. Escudero. Phoenix: Ultreya Press, 1964.

———. *Questions and Problems Concerning Cursillos in Christianity.* Translated by W. Young. Phoenix: Ultreya Press, 1966.

Hobsbawn, E. *Primitive Rebels.* New York: Norton and Company, 1965.

Howard, R. "Prose for Borges." In *Prose for Borges.* Edited by C. Newman and M. Kinzie. Evanston: Northwestern University Press, 1972.

Hymes, D. "Introduction: Toward Ethnographies of Communication." In *The Ethnography of Communication.* Edited by J. Gumperz and D. Hymes. Menasha, Wisconsin: American Anthropological Association, 1964.

———. *Reinventing Anthropology.* New York: Vintage Books, 1974.

Izquierdo, P. "The Psychology of the Newly Converted in the Cursillo." Mimeographed, n.d.

Jacobs, W. "God's Plan For His People." In *Proceedings of the Sixth National Conference—Cursillos in Christianity.* Phoenix: Ultreya Press, 1965.

Jarvie, I. *Revolution in Anthropology.* London: Routledge and Kegan Paul, 1964.

Bibliography

———. "Theories of Cargo Cults: A Critical Analysis." *Oceania* 34 (1963).

Kaplan, A. *The Conduct of Inquiry: Methodology for Behavioral Science.* San Francisco: Chandler Publishing Company, 1964.

Kenyatta, J. "Kikuyu Religion, Ancestor Worship and Sacrificial Practices." *Africa* 10 (1937).

Kierkegaard, S. *Fear and Trembling and the Sickness unto Death.* Translated by W. Lowrie. Princeton: Princeton University Press, 1941.

———. *Philosophical Fragments.* Translated by D. Swenson. Princeton: Princeton University Press, 1941.

Kopytoff, I. "African Religious Movements: Indigenous Versus Acculturative Factors." Master's thesis. Northwestern University, 1963.

Kuhn, T. *The Structure of Scientific Revolution.* Chicago: The University of Chicago Press, 1962.

La Barre, W. "Materials for a History of Studies of Crisis Cults: A Bibliographic Essay." *Current Anthropology* 12, no. 1 (1971).

Lange, J. *The Cognitivity Paradox—An Inquiry Concerning the Claims of Philosophy.* Princeton: Princeton University Press, 1970.

Lawrence, P. *Road Belong Cargo: A Study of the Cargo Movement in the Southern Madang District.* Manchester: Manchester University Press, 1964.

Leach, E. *Rethinking Anthropology.* London: Athlone Press, 1961.

Leeson, I. "Bibliography of Cargo Cults and Other Nativistic Movements in the South Pacific." Sydney: South Pacific Commission, Technical Paper 30, 1952.

Levi-Strauss, C. *Structural Anthropology.* New York: Doubleday and Company, 1963.

———. *The Savage Mind.* London: Weidenfield and Nicholson, 1966.

Lewis, O. *Life in a Mexican Village: Tepoztlan Restudied.* Urbana: University of Illinois Press, 1960.

Linton, R. "Nativistic Movements." *American Anthropologist* 44 (1943).

Mair, L. "Independent Religious Movements in Three Continents." *Comparative Studies in Society and History* 1 (1959).

———. "The Pursuit of the Millenium in Melanesia." *British Journal of Sociology* 9 (1958).

Malinowski, B. *Argonauts of the Western Pacific.* New York: E. P. Dutton and Company, 1961.

Manion, T. and DeTar, J. *To Deceive . . . the Elect.* Reno: Athanasius Press, 1969.

Mannheim, K. *Ideology and Utopia.* New York: Harcourt, Brace and World, 1936.

Maquet, J. "Objectivity in Anthropology." In *Current Anthropology* 5 (1964).

———. *The Sociology of Knowledge.* Translated by J. Locke. Boston: Beacon Press, 1951.

Marías, J. *Metaphysical Anthropology: The Empirical Structure of Human Life.* Translated by F. Lopez-Morillas. Univeristy Park: The Pennsylvania State Univerity Press, 1971.

Mead, M. "Ritual and Social Crisis." In *The Roots of Ritual.* Edited by J. Shaughnessey. Grand Rapids: W. B. Eerdmans, 1973.

McCall, G. and Simmons, J. *Issues in Participant Observation.* Reading: Addison-Wesley, 1969.

Bibliography

Merleau-Ponty, M. *The Prose of the World.* Translated by J. O'Neill. Evanston: Northwestern University Press, 1973.
———. *Signs.* Translated by R. McCleary. Evanston: Northwestern University Press, 1964.
Metraux, A. *Voodoo in Haiti.* Translated by H. Charteris. New York: Schocken Books, 1972.
Mills, C. Wright. *The Sociological Imagination.* New York: Grove Press, 1961.
Minkowski, E. *Lived Time: Phenomenology and Psychopathological Studies.* Translated by N. Metzel. Evanston: Northwestern University Press, 1970.
Mitchell, R. and Turner, B., compilers. *A Bibliography of Modern African Religious Movements.* Evanston: Northwestern University Press, 1966.
National Secretariat of Venezuela. *The Fundamental Ideas of the Cursillo Movement.* Dallas: National Ultreya Publications, 1974.
Nietsche, F. *The Gay Science.* Translated by W. Kaufman. New York: Vintage Books, 1974.
Norbeck, E. *Religion in Primitive Society.* Evanston: Harper and Row, 1961.
O'Neill, J. Translator's Introduction, "Language and the Voice of Philosophy." In *The Prose of the World,* by M. Merleau-Ponty. Evanston: Northwestern University Press, 1973.
Parson, T. *The Structure of Social Action.* Glencoe: The Free Press, 1968.
Pelto, P. *Anthropological Research: The Structure of Inquiry.* New York: Harper and Row, 1970.
Quine, W. *Ontological Relativity and Other Essays.* New York: Columbia University Press, 1969.

Radcliffe-Brown, A. *Structure and Function in Primitive Society*. New York: The Free Press, 1952.
Radin, P. *Primitive Religion*. New York: Viking Press, 1937.
Redfield, R. *Tepoztlan—A Mexican Village*. Chicago: University of Chicago Press, 1930.
Ribeiro, R. "Brazilian Messianic Movements." In *Millenial Dreams in Action*. Edited by S. Thrupp. The Hague: Mouton, 1962.
Rohloff, I. *The Origins and Development of Cursillo*. Dallas: National Ultreya Publications, 1976.
Sartre, J. *What is Literature?* Translated by B. Frechtman. New York: Washington Square Press, 1966.
Scheler, M. *The Nature of Sympathy*. P. Heath. Hamden: Archon Books, 1970.
Schutz, A. *Collected Papers I: The Problem of Social Reality*. The Hague: Martinus Nijhoff, 1967.
Slaatte, H. *The Pertinence of the Paradox: Dialectics of Reason-In-Existence*. New York: Humanities Press, 1968.
Stein, M. *The Eclipse of Community*. New York: Harper and Row, 1964.
Steiner, G. *Language and Silence*. New York: Atheneum, 1972.
Stevens, W. *Poems*. New York: Vintage Books, 1959.
Sundkler, B. *Bantu Prophets in South Africa*. New York: Oxford University Press, 1961.
Talmon, Y. "Pursuit of the Millenium: The Relation Between Religious and Social Change." *European Journal of Sociology* 3 (1962).
Tempels, P. *Bantu Philosophy*. Paris: Présence Africaine, 1959.

Bibliography

Turner, V. *The Forest of Symbols.* Ithaca: Cornell University Press, 1967.

———. *The Ritual Process: Structure and Antistructure.* Chicago: Aldine Press, 1969.

Valéry, P. *The Art of Poetry.* Translated by D. Folliot. New York: Pantheon Books, 1958.

Vann Gennep, A. *The Rites of Passage.* Chicago: Phoenix Books, 1960.

Wagner, R. *The Curse of Souw.* Chicago: The University of Chicago Press, 1967.

———. *The Invention of Culture.* Englewood Cliffs: Prentice-Hall, 1975.

Wallace, A. *Religion: An Anthropological View.* New York: Random House, 1966.

———. "Revitalization Movements." *American Anthropologist* 58 (1956).

Weber, M. *The Sociology of Religion.* Translated by E. Fischoff. Boston: Beacon Press, 1964.

———. *The Theory of Social and Economic Organization.* Translated by T. Parsons. New York: The Free Press, 1964.

Williams, F. *Orokaiva Magic.* London: Oxford University Press, 1928.

———. "The Vailala Madness and the Destruction of Native Ceremonies in the Gulf Division." Port Moresby: *Papuan Anthropology Reports* 4 (1923).

Wisdom, J. *Paradox and Discovery.* Berkeley: University of California Press, 1970.

Wolff, K. *Trying Sociology.* New York: John Wiley and Sons, 1974.

———. *Surrender and Catch: Experience and Inquiry Today.* Boston: Reidel, 1976.

Worsley, P. *The Trumpet Shall Sound: A Study of "Cargo" Cults in Melanesia.* New York: Schocken Books, 1968.

INDEX

"Action," 77, 79
Africa, 24, 25, 166, 194
Albrecht, Fidelis, 26
Arizona, Phoenix, 25
Arizona, Tucson, 25
Augustine, 108
Ave Maria, 153
Azores, Ponta Delgada, 224

Barthes, Roland, 177
Bonnin, Edouardo, 8, 9, 10, 11, 12, 13, 14, 15, 17, 18, 19, 20, 22, 23, 24, 25, 30, 31, 52, 144, 145, 165, 166, 167, 170, 172, 180, 192, 193, 194, 196, 199, 200, 201, 202, 203, 209, 221, 237, 263
Brovana, Greg, 209, 210
Burridge, K., 165, 197
Burke, Kenneth, 199

Capo, Juan, 18, 20
Catholic Action, 14, 16, 17, 18, 19
Chardin, Teilhard de, 108
"Christian Community", 93, 94
"Christian Life", 93, 94
Christian Program for Personal Improvement, 124
Clark, Tom, 172
Clark, Stephen, 164
clausura, 29
Cuba, 17
Cuidad Real, 21, 22, 24, 209, 224
cummings, e.e., 243
"The Curcillo Movement", 141

Cursillos in Christianity — Instrument of Christian Renewal, 30

de colores, 29, 125, 222, 223, 252, 256
decuria, 72, 73, 102, 256
Derrida, J., 219, 220
De Tar, John, 150, 151, 152

Eliot, T.S., 102, 120, 231
Enciso, Jesus, 21, 146

Father Cicero, 204
Fernandez, Gabriel, 25
"The Fourth Day", 93, 95, 96
Franco, Francisco, 7, 21, 22

"Grace", 74, 75
Geertz, C, 4, 182
"Group and Ultreya", 93, 95

Harris, Martin, 134
Heidegger, Martin, 49, 218, 269
Hervas, Juan, 13, 14, 15, 16, 17, 18, 19, 20, 21, 22, 23, 24, 25, 28, 29, 30, 31, 40, 52, 56, 136, 141, 144, 149, 164, 165, 166, 168, 170, 172, 193, 194, 196, 197, 199, 200, 201, 202, 203, 204, 206, 207, 208, 209, 221, 222, 224, 237, 253, 263
Holy Name Society, 136
Hölderlin, 239
"The Holy Spirit", 74, 75

"Ideal", 74

Index

Illinois, Chicago, 17, 224, 225
Inter-American Congress of Social Action, 17
International Federation of Catholic Men, 208
Izquierdo, P., 104

Jacobs, William J., 153, 154

Kimbangu, Simon, 204
Knights of Columbus, 136, 144
"Know Yourself", 66, 76

"Laymen in the Church", 74, 75
"Leaders", 77, 80
Leaders' Manual for Cursillos in Christianity, 30
Leaders' School, 43, 45, 46, 48, 54, 185, 242, 257
Legion of Mary, 144
Lewis, Oscar, 266
Luther, Martin, 204

McCall, G, 253
Mambu, 195, 199, 202, 204
Malinowski, B., 251
Mallorca, 7, 8, 9, 11, 12, 13, 14, 15, 17, 19, 20, 21, 22, 23, 24, 25, 29, 30, 31, 36, 52, 79, 87, 112, 145, 146, 149, 166, 192, 209, 221, 224
Manion, Thomas, 150, 151, 152
Maquet, Jacques, 267
Marlas, J., 143
Massachusetts, Boston, 224

Merleau-Ponty, M., 86, 87
Michigan, Lansing, 26, 224
Minkowski, E., 170
Muntzer, Thomas, 204

New Mexico, Sante Fe, 25
New Testament, 6, 13, 237
New York, New York, 17, 26
Nietzche, Frederick, 169

"Obstacles to a Life in Christ", 77, 80
Ohio, Lorain, 25
Ohio, Toledo, 17

palanca, 29, 81, 82, 84, 85, 86, 88, 90, 96, 102, 256
Palomino, Augustin, 25
Pelto, P., 268
"Piety", 74, 75
Pilgrim Captains, 8, 9, 10
Pilgrim Scouts, 8, 9, 10
Pius X, 17
Pius XII, 17, 207, 208
precursillo, 36, 43, 46
"The Prodigal Son", 67, 68

Questions and Problems Concerning Cursillos in Christianity, 30

Redfield, Robert, 266
Reformation, 108
Rohloff, I., 19
rollo, 29, 45, 51, 72, 72, 73, 74, 76, 77, 79, 80, 86, 89, 93, 94, 95, 96, 102, 134, 256

"Sacraments", 77, 79
St. James the Greater, 8, 9
Santiago de Compostela, 8, 9, 10, 211
San Honorato, 9, 10, 11, 18, 19
Sartre, J, 195
Schutz, Alfred, 86
Segui, Padre, 19, 20
Simmons, J., 253
Spanish Pontifical College, 208
Stein, Maurice, 253
Steiner, George, 203
Stevens, Wallace, 135
"Study", 77, 78
"Study and Christian Learning of the Environment", 93

Temples, Placide, 166, 194, 198, 204
Texas, Amarillo, 25
Texas, Lackland Air Force Base, 25
Texas, San Angelo, 25, 26
Texas, Waco, 25
"The Three Glances at Christ", 68

Thomas, W.I., 139
Torres, Bartolome, 21
"Total Security", 95

ultreya, 21, 29, 93, 95, 124, 125, 126, 145, 146, 152, 222, 252
University of Freiburg, 17

Valencia, Diocese of, 17
Valéry, Paul, 269
Vatican II, 59, 112, 113, 136, 147, 168, 256
Vadell, Bernado, 25

"What You Should Know When You Make a Cursillo", 55
World War II, 7
Workshop of Christian Leadership, 77
Workshop of Christian Learning, 50
Workshop in Christian Living, 45

Yali, 204